WATERFORD MEMORIES
150 years with the *Munster Express*

Dedicated to the former Editors
and to all our readers

WATERFORD MEMORIES

150 years with the
Munster Express
Edited by
Kieran Walsh

A. & A. Farmar

British Library Cataloguing in Publication Data
A CIP catalogue record for this book is available
from the British Library

ISBN: 978-1-906353-18-6

This edition first published in 2010
by
A. & A. Farmar Ltd
78 Ranelagh Village, Dublin 6, Ireland
Tel +353-1-496 3625 Fax +353-1-497 0107
Email afarmar@iol.ie
Web aafarmar.ie

Printed and bound by ColourBooks
Typeset and designed by Bookworks

Contents

Acknowledgements

We wish to thank the following:
For written contributions:
Dermot Keyes, Myriam Walsh, Tom Young, John O'Connor, Liam Murphy, Michael Dower, Michael Comerford, Anthony Brophy, Donal Barry, Matt Keane, the late Mick Browne, the late Seamus Grant, Norman Freeman, Davy Walsh, Fintan Walsh, Hugh Oram, Jim Burke, Joe Falvey, Brian Nolan, Joe Malone, John Goff, junior

For illustrations:
Donal Moore, Waterford City Archives, Eoin Murphy, Leo Murphy, Breda Mc Grath, the late Joe McGrath, the Jack O Neill photo collection, the National Library of Ireland, Philip Martin of Irish Newspaper Archives

For scanning from the original newspapers:
Eilish McGrath, Emma Walsh, Joe Dalton, Seán Maher

Editorial input:
Waterford City Library, Tony and Anna Farmar

Other contributions:
Cllr Davy Daniels, Cllr Davy Walsh, Cllr Mary Roche, Evan Musgrave, Walsh family members, especially Roswitha, Priscilla, Myriam, Christoph and Killian.
All those who appeared in the *Munster Express* 150th anniversary show, especially producer Michael Grant, Jim Nolan and Nicola Beresford and the Theatre Royal.

J. J. Walsh remembered

When he died in 1992, J. J. Walsh hoped that a history of the newspaper he loved and worked for so long would be published on the 150th anniversary. It is fitting therefore that he be specially remembered.

J. J. Walsh was editor of the *Munster Express* for over 50 years. He successfully steered the newspaper through some of the most tumultuous times of the 20th century.

Anecdotes and stories about him have been part of Waterford folklore for years, though most of them are untrue. In fact, not too many people knew him well on a personal basis because he kept himself to himself a great deal and he outlived most of his friends and peers.

He worked hard and expected others to do the same and he happily admitted to being an eccentric. That said, perhaps, it was his often unorthodox approach that made him successful in business.

He once agreed, during a television interview, that it would not be too far off the mark to describe him as a 'conservative, right wing Catholic'. He was, after all, the only Irish editor to attend the funeral of the Spanish leader, General Franco. When he heard that Franco's death was imminent, he walked into the city offices of Harvey Travel and told the startled managing director, Seán Power, to monitor the radio news and, as soon as the announcement was made, to make all the necessary arrangements for his trip to Madrid.

Despite his own firm views, the pages of the *Munster Express* were open to all manner of opinion and beliefs. It was sometimes alleged that only people whose views were similar to J. J. Walsh's received decent coverage in the newspaper but that was simply not true. I often saw him angrily remonstrating about the content of interviews and reports but he never attempted to suppress such views. 'We provide a level pitch and everybody is welcome to play,' was one of his favourite sayings.

Mr Walsh was always an innovator who eagerly embraced new technology and he lived long enough to help develop the computer age in his newspaper. He loved the cacophony of the printing works that set adrenalin flowing and, sometimes, mischief as well. He was happy amid the spitting and hissing of the old hot metal days, the clanking and clanging of the Linotypes, the banging of mallets on huge frames of type and the high-pitched machine gun rattle of the old Cossar flatbed press as it spewed out the latest edition.

But he knew that to stand still was to fall behind and he wouldn't have been too sentimental about change. Nevertheless, I can't help but wonder what he would make of today's newspaper where the predominant sound is the dull clunk-clunk sound of computer keyboards over a soft whirl of mainframes and the murmur of calm voices.

Mr Walsh died in 1992 and his going really did mark the end of an era.

John O'Connor, News Editor, *Munster Express*

Some books used in the course of compiling this volume

H. Fyle & A. T. Newham *The Waterford and Tramore Railway*

John Gaule *Butler or Blood*

Harvey's *Directory of Waterford*

Brian Havel *Maestro of Crystal*

Bill Irish *Shipbuilding in Waterford 1820–1882*

Emmet O'Connor *Labour History of Waterford*

John O'Connor *The Munster, the Music and the Village*

Jack O'Neill *Waterford: its history and people*

Vincent Power *Send 'em Home S weatin'*

A. Taylor *Tramore AFC 1952–2002*

J. J. Walsh *Across the World for Sport*

J. J. Walsh *Waterford Yesterdays and Tomorrows*

PART ONE
1860–1910

1860—A year of prosperity

In July 1860, the month the *Munster Express* was launched, the Solicitor General rose to address a court in Belfast, where several men were being prosecuted for sectarian attacks. This is what he said:

'Unwonted tranquillity prevails in Ireland. There is peace in her homesteads, and security for property and life throughout the great majority of her counties. The jails are comparatively empty; the convict prisons have fewer inmates than at any former time; the judges are relieved of much of their labour in repressing civil discord, and generally they can congratulate the grand juries on the improving condition of the kingdom.'

Ireland's steady recovery from the prostration of the Famine seemed extraordinary to contemporaries. As the chief government statistician put it some years later: 'It may be that Ireland has recovered from a condition of almost wreck more completely than any other country would have done'. The key was the rapidly growing industrial cities of England, which were hungry for all the meat, the butter and the wheat that Ireland could supply. And a good proportion of that produce went through Waterford, one of Ireland's major ports at the time. By the time of the Land War of the 1880s, Ireland's special position was being undermined by Swedish, Danish and French butter and bacon and American and Australian meat and wheat.

A view of Waterford from Misery Hill (Courtesy National Library of Ireland)

Waterford in the 1860s

Harvey's *Directory* was the very first trade guide book to Waterford, published in 1866, just six years after the first edition of the *Munster Express*.

Waterford city had a population about half its current level, at 22,778. At the time, the city was connected with Ferrybank by way of a timber bridge that had 39 arches and was a massive 832 feet in length—'Timbertoes' as it was called. This bridge had been opened in January 1794, and tolls were still being profitably collected from anyone who wished to cross.

According to Harvey's *Directory* the principal manufacturing activity was brewing and bacon curing with some distilling. The city had three breweries, four foundries and several flour mills.

The main public buildings were religious, including the Catholic and Protestant cathedrals, five Catholic chapels, and four convents. As well as this there were Presbyterian, Baptist, Methodist, Independent and Friends' meeting houses. There was the Catholic College of St John for the

The Imperial power on display as a troop of soldiers provides an honour guard to the Assize Judge as he leaves the Judge's Residence (now the location of the new Tower Hotel) next to the Imperial Hotel (Courtesy National Library of Ireland)

education of the clergy and the Christian Brothers Mount Sion School, educating over 1,000 boys. There was also a model school, a blue coat school, a diocesan school and a Protestant Hall plus a Catholic High School for those going on to university.

The Waterford Court House stands where it is today and for offenders there was a house of correction, and a substantial gaol, near Ballybricken market, whose wall loomed over the terraces of small houses.

The Customs House, on Adelphi Quay, City Hall and the Savings Bank on O'Connell Street were other fine public buildings as well as the Chamber of Commerce Building on Georges Street.

Like all towns in Ireland at the time, Waterford made as much as could be made in the city. The rush of manufactured goods from Britain, which the railways made so easy, had barely started.

There were twenty dressmakers, as well as hatters, milliners, shoemakers and silk mercers. Other trades that supplied the town were soap and candle makers, rope makers, gunmakers, hemp merchants, lamp manufacturers, lead merchants, an Italian Warehouse (selling

Tranquil days in O'Connell Street (Courtesy National Library of Ireland)

Italian olive oil, groceries and fruits), feather merchants, cutlers, dyers and carvers.

For the farming community there were grain and seed merchants, poulterers, and game dealers and farm tools providers. There was even a guano merchant, importing the wonder fertiliser of the nineteenth century (which is basically bird-droppings). This remained popular until artificial fertiliser came in in the 1900s. As it happened, the farming industry in Waterford was gradually responding to market demand from Britain and turning its arable land to pasture.

Just as today, numerous of the building trades were represented, from builders to stone masons, cabinet makers and upholsterers to furniture makers, plumbers and gas fitters, painters, civil engineers, and timber merchants such as Graves and Dowleys with Penrose of Rose Lane.

The drinks trade was also well represented, especially spirit dealers and wine merchants. As befitted a major port there was a large export and import trade in drink from historical times and this was reflected here. Ale and porter were generally supplied then in barrels by the brewer and bottled in the cellar by the publican or other retailer. The brewers were Cherry Brothers, King Street (now O'Connell Street), Davis and Strangman, at Mary Street (now the Brewery), as well as Keily on New Street. To cater for this trade more than a dozen specialist coopers or barrel makers were listed, as well as cork manufacturers.

Specialist port businesses included ship owners and brokers, ship builders, such as Cox on the Quay and Angell on Hanover Street, chandlers, sail makers, salt merchants and salmon exporters, such as Kenny on the High Street.

A picture, in fact, of a bustling, busy, but self-contained community.

The old fish market in Peter Street 1890 (Courtesy J. O' Neill collection)

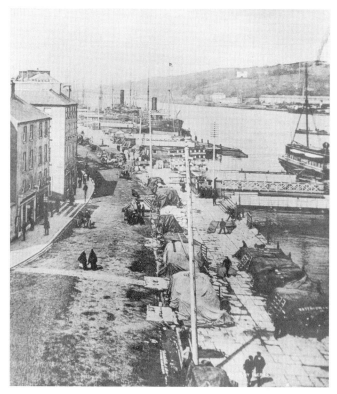

A busy scene at the Quays (Courtesy J. O' Neill collection)

The fair on the Hill of Ballybricken 1897
(Courtesy J. O' Neill collection)

The Market House on the Quays in the early 1900s
(Courtesy J. O' Neill collection)

Another view of Ballybricken fair. The trade in pigs was especially prominent, and the farm wives would sell their eggs, poultry and butter. Being untreated, the fair ground was muddy and uneven in bad weather. (Courtesy J. O' Neill collection)

The first edition of the *Munster Express*

The very first edition of the *Munster Express* was dated Saturday 7 July 1860. In its twelve pages it covered Irish and international news—the latter unashamedly 'lifted' from British publications, as was the custom of the time. Twelve pages does not sound much, but the type was densely set, with very little relief for the eye in the way of headlines. The number of words was not much less than the modern multi-section paper.

The front page was devoted to ads, mostly for shipping companies, but also for the fashionable shop of Robertson, Ledlie, Ferguson & Co. at 53 The Quay (now Shaw's) , where July fashions and 'elegant personal requisites' could be obtained.

Inside there was racing news from the Curragh and from Epsom. Page three covered news and market intelligence from nearby counties, Limerick, Wexford, Tipperary and Carlow.

The big crime story of the day was the sensational Road Hill House case in Somerset, England, described in the paper as 'a most cruel and mysterious murder'. Part of the sensation arose from the fact that the murdered child's half-sister and half-brother were suspected of the gruesome killing. (This crime was the subject of a 2008 best-seller called *The Suspicions of Mr Whicher*. And yes, many years later the sister confessed and was imprisoned for twenty years.)

In Dungarvan a 'gang of ruffians' had attempted to rob a bank, but were thwarted. Denny's had just invented a new method of singeing pigs, and in Cork a 'stout, buxom

servant girl' called Mary Hooley had fractured her collarbone while engaged in romps with a fellow-servant.

And of course there were fashions—flounces were back, the readers were told, and 'huge open sleeves will be generally adopted'.

The range of foreign news is impressive. There are stories from Spain, France, Austria, Switzerland, Russia, Turkey and Japan (here the Emperor had just been assassinated. In reprisal thirty of his bodyguard were beheaded and two Princes of the Blood permitted to disembowel themselves). The big foreign news was Garibaldi's triumphs in Sicily (as pictured in the Charlton Heston

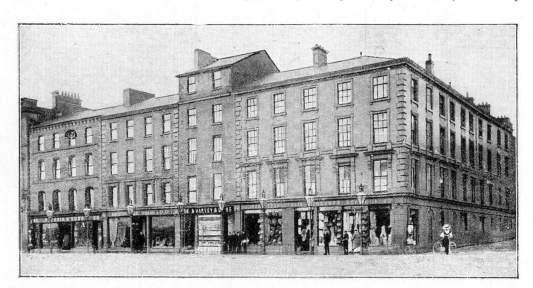

This block of buildings represents the continued growth of nearly three quarter's of a century's progress

Furniture Manufacturers. Removals Executed with Complete satisfaction.

General Drapers and Outfitters.

WATERFORD'S FASHION CENTRE.

Robertson, Ledlie, Ferguson & Co., Ltd.,
BELFAST, WATERFORD, AND CORK.

The old department store of Robertson, Ledlie, Ferguson & Co. (now Shaw's) was an advertiser from the very first edition of the Munster Express.

film *The Leopard*). Because Garibaldi's attempt to unify the country threatened the Papal lands in the middle of Italy, he was much less popular in Ireland than in England. Indeed, the *Munster Express* reported that seventy Irishmen were spotted in Boulogne on their way to defend the Pope in Rome against the insurgents, just as 75 years later Waterfordmen were to go to Spain to defend their religion with General Franco.

All this for four old pence, which, if we take inflation into account, is probably about the same as the €2.00 the much expanded paper costs today. And if that was a stretch, you could always join a sharing group, as an old Master of the Rotunda remembered the frugal newspaper-readers of his youth in the 1860s used to do. 'As four pence a day', Dr Atthill wrote in his autobiography, 'was a heavy tax on persons of limited means, there was a regular trade established for the lending of it at a penny per hour. One person got it, say at eight o' clock; it would be called for at nine o' clock when his neighbour had it, and so on; or you could buy one of these copies in the afternoon for twopence.' (Dr Lombe Atthill, *Recollections of an Irish Doctor* (1911) p 114.)

Live turkeys for sale, a few weeks before Christmas (Courtesy National Library of Ireland)

The last public execution in Waterford

The last time a man was hanged in public in Waterford was on 14 April 1864. Not long after this, public execution was finally abolished throughout Britain and Ireland. The last man to be publicly executed in London was the Fenian Michael Barret, in what many still believe to have been a miscarriage of justice.

The last public hanging in Waterford followed the brutal murder of an elderly farmer called Thomas Connolly. Mr Connolly's grandson, Patrick Hennessy, lived with him and in time the young man married a Bridget Walsh. The marriage settlement allowed for Bridget's parents to live in Mr Connolly's house with the young couple and the older man. The arrangement went well for a time but bickering led Mrs Walsh to leave, never to return.

On the morning of 29 September, 1863, the only occupants of the lonely cottage were Connolly, Thomas Walsh and young Bridget. Bridget went to the well for water and on return met a shocking sight—her father standing over the badly wounded Connolly and nearby a blood-covered hatchet. Walsh dismembered and buried the body parts but all was discovered. Nearly seven months later Thomas Walsh was hanged, one of two men executed for murder in Ireland that year. (For comparison there were 21 people hanged in Britain that year, including the five 'Flowery Land' mutineers. Britain's population was about 24 million at this date, compared to Ireland's 5.6 million.)

Public hangings took place outside the gaol at Ballybricken, on the rise above the Garda Station. Between two and three thousand people gathered to witness the event. Military and police were also in attendance.

High Street in the 1920s

'Walsh,' wrote one reporter, 'with beads in his right hand, walked firmly from his cell between Fathers Dunphy and McGrath, both wearing their stoles and reciting the Litany.'

In a short time the executioner pinioned Walsh's arms to his side, bound them with strong twine and then covered his head with a white cap. When the white cap was seen by the assembled people 'a moan of horror was emitted.'

At ten minutes past eight 'the wretched man reached the scaffold' and the executioner took the rope 'and placed the noose around the culprit's neck.' When the executioner removed the pin to release the trap, it did not work. The Governor 'with most commendable foresight' had a sledgehammer in hand and 'this was now put into requisition.' The executioner applied it and on the third blow the trap gave way and 'the unfortunate man was hurled into eternity.'

The Waterford Bicycle Club before the introduction of the 'safety bicycle' (Courtesy National Library of Ireland)

The original proprietors, the Fisher family

The Fishers originally came from Scotland and had settled in Youghal. Joseph Fisher took over the 30-year-old *Waterford Daily Mail* in 1853. Fisher was a Protestant, but of very liberal views, and his ideas became increasingly nationalist, so much so that a rival paper the *Waterford Standard* was founded to express Ascendancy views.

These papers were essentially Waterford City publications. To cater for the farmers and country people outside the city Fisher launched in 1860 the *Munster Express*. The *Munster Express* started in New Street, Waterford, off Michael Street and John Street. Liberal in politics, the

Munster Express newspaper was admired by Isaac Butt, the leader of the nationalist group in Westminister before Parnell.

Joseph Fisher died in 1882, and his sons took over the business. However, the papers got into difficulties and in 1907 they sold both the *Munster Express* and *Waterford Daily Mail* to a rising politician and businessman in Waterford called Edward Walsh. His family have run the *Munster Express* ever since.

Walsh later bought the *Kilkenny and Wexford Express*, the small County Tipperary *Independent* and the *Tipperary Free Press* which was published in Clonmel until 1892. In 1907 Edward Walsh added to his empire by acquiring the daily *Waterford Citizen* (founded 1859).

At this time a threat emerged from Dublin as the newly re-activated *Irish Independent*, owned by William Martin Murphy, began to reach Waterford in the morning, thus directly competing with the *Citizen*. In the face of this threat—for the *Independent* not only carried hot national news, but was also cheaper than any of Walsh's papers— he combined all the papers into one, creating a city newspaper plus county paper, giving the *Munster Express* a regional edge to its circulation, and making it larger against the opposition.

So the *Munster Express* became a larger local circulation paper rivalling not only the *Irish Independent* but also the local *Waterford News*, *Waterford Star* and the *Waterford Standard*, the old ascendancy title, later to be acquired by the *Munster Express* in the early 1960s.

A very successful newspaper business was now operating from the Quay premises.

The Protestant Hall on Catherine Street

Bakehouse Lane 1890

Waterford in the Land War

In Waterford city there was doubt where the sympathies of most of the voters lay. They consistently elected Nationalist and Home Rule MPs, and in December 1880 presented the freedom of the city to Charles Stewart Parnell, the leader of the Irish Party.

When he visited the city to receive the honour, he addressed a monster meeting in Ballybricken, flanked by banners declaring 'Parnell, Ireland's future President' and 'All Hail to the Chief'. To cheers, he declared his belief that the back of English rule in Ireland was broken and that the country would regain its legislative independence. It was noted by the unionist *Waterford Standard*, however, that few of the city's labouring class attended this rally with its

Broad Street in the early 1900s. Although the shops are open, the town clearly does not suffer from a traffic problem.
(Courtesy National Library of Ireland)

exclusive attention to rural matters. The poor housing and labour conditions of Waterford citizens were not on the agenda.

The vote in favour of Parnell in the council was not a walk-over. Considerable opposition was mounted by the unionists. These 'no' voters were subsequently boycotted, and had windows smashed in their shops and business premises. They were subsequently actively encouraged to follow the general example and decorate their buildings with flags to greet Parnell.

Many of the city leaders were deeply active in the Land League, not least Joseph Fisher of the *Munster Express* who had been a leading member of the Farmers' Club. After a major rally in support of tenants evicted by Lord Waterford, Fisher gave a rousing speech outside the Court House denouncing the events.

Waterford was near enough to the country to make it practical for the Hunt to meet on the Adelphi Quay (Courtesy National Library of Ireland).

Fisher was a Poor Law Guardian, and the unions became a major battlefield for the struggle between the League and the landlords. A major tactic was to disrupt the landlords' hunting. In 1881 the Carrick-on-Suir branch of the League resolved to prevent all hunting in Waterford. These were violent days—rumours circulated of hounds being poisoned, and certainly landlords found it was imprudent to declare in advance where they might be going. This was largely a rural battle, however; in the city things were generally quiet, with only one assault and one case of intimidation in the first half of 1881. This hectic stage of the Land War was brought to an end in 1882.

The old railway station on the Dublin–Kilkenny line (Courtesy J. O' Neill collection)

Munster Express Editor jailed

In September 1889 the Editor of the *Munster Express*, William Garrow Fisher, son of the original founder, was jailed for reporting a meeting of the Land League.

In the battle against rack-rents in the late 1880s, the Land League's great weapon was the boycott. In the close-knit Irish society of the day this was a deadly sanction. So successful was it that the government under Chief Secretary Arthur Balfour passed a Coercion Act, called the Perpetual Crimes Act 1887, designed to outlaw boycotting and threats of boycotting.

The new law meant that anyone supporting the tactics of the Land League against landlords was vulnerable. Many famous names found themselves in prison as a result, including Parnell, Willie Redmond and Michael Davitt. Not least of those prosecuted under the Act was the second Editor of the *Munster Express* William Fisher.

An apple seller snug in her box, complete with her short pipe, known as a 'jaw-warmer' or 'dudeen'. (Courtesy J. O' Neill collection)

Fisher was a strong supporter of Parnell and the Land League. It is difficult now to realise how radical this was. But for many, including the Pope, who condemned the tactics of the League in an Encyclical of 1888, the Land League's urging of 'No Rents' was effectively calling for an abandonment of private property altogether, or at least the nationalisation of the land. Conservatives feared that if a farmer could be ostracised for simply paying rents he could well afford, for fulfilling his legal obligations, the whole basis of contract law would be undermined.

So when William Fisher was sent to prison in 1889 for an offence against the Act he was not especially surprised, and neither were his readers. His offence was to report the proceedings of the Stradbally branch of the Irish National League (as the Land League was then called) in which resolutions denouncing a Matthew Whelan as a land-grabber were debated. The paper reported that there had been a debate as to whether Whelan should be put on the black list, i.e. boycotted. The court decided that merely reporting this discussion amount to intimidation, and the Editor was sentenced to 14 days in Waterford Gaol.

From there he was able to write in high style and indignation. 'His crime, forsooth, was that in this his own paper he published a report of a meeting. This has been the awful offence for which he today has to associate with the elite of the Waterford slums, and with the scourings of the scum of society.' But as the paper reported elsewhere, the Editor bore up well under his ordeal, being regularly visited in prison by the Mayor and other Nationalists.

In the grand manner of the day he declared his certainty that 'no weak-kneed tyranny, backed up with crooked malice, and supported by every engine of devilry, no modern Cromwellian tactics, prompted by base and brutish motives, no battering ram policy, whether applied to individuals or peasants' homes, in a word no coercion, however strong, will eradicate the strong and inherent love of the Irish people for the old land, and no imprisonment or persecution will break a spirit that has withstood the storms of centuries.'

William Fisher left Ireland for America after his prison term and his brother Harry ran the paper until he sold it in 1907 to Edward Walsh.

The rise and fall of the Malcolmsons

Because the city of Waterford had been tolerant to the Quakers in the early 1700s, many business families with Quaker connections settled in the city. Among these are families whose names ring down the years in Waterford industry—Penrose, Pim, Grubb, Strangman, Jacobs and Goff. But the mightiest of these, certainly in the nineteenth century, was the Malcolmson family.

They had begun in the corn and flour trade, but by 1826 had expanded into cotton, establishing a substantial mill on the Suir. The business thrived, employing 1,500 workers by 1853. There was also Modeltown, Portlaw, with a population of four thousand. The Malcolmsons were tough employers, setting demanding work schedules, and their village was designed (like Jeremy Bentham's ideal prison) in radial mode so a single policeman could stand in the centre and oversee every house. Specially wide streets were designed to facilitate the workers going to and from the factory. A no-smoking rule was strictly enforced. But they also provided gas lighting for the streets, a school, a factory doctor, a savings bank, a cooperative store and reading rooms.

All this activity, with coal and raw cotton coming in to the factory and finished goods going out, meant that shipping was an essential part of the operation. By the 1830s Malcolmson's owned over two hundred boats of all sorts to handle the trade. Around this time they founded the Waterford Steam Navigation Company, which soon ran several massive paddle-steamers trading with Bristol, Liverpool and London as well as Irish ports. Iron was then the new material, and in the 1840s Malcolmsons established the Neptune Ironworks to make and repair iron-hulled vessels.

The first ship built was the SS *Neptune,* over 300 tons, launched in 1846. For the next thirty years, riding a world boom in shipping, the Neptune works built an iron steamship every year, the largest of which were produced in the 1860s, including the SS *Cella* (1796 tons), the SS *Iowa* (1781 tons) and the SS *William Penn* (1799 tons) all built for the London–New York route.

O'Connell Street 1900

In 1858, at the height of the company's prosperity, the inititiator of all this activity, the shrewd Joseph Malcolmson, died. The company, with its extended interests and investments, had become one of the largest steamship proprietors in the world, as well as runnning cotton, coal and other businesses. Its ships ran to St Petersburg and the Baltic, to Rotterdam and Bremen, to Brazil and the River Plate, and to China and India. Waterford was much more significant in world shipping than Belfast.

But this extraordinary success was not to last. Joseph Malcolmson's heirs, notably his brother William, who became senior partner, had nothing like his entrepreneurial acuteness, and a series of disasters rapidly brought the mighty firm to its knees. William began by establishing the Galway Line to supply the government's transatlantic mail service. Unfortunately, the paddle steamers he commissioned for the Line (to meet overly stringent contractual conditions) were speedy but not strong enough to cope with the severe conditions of the north Atlantic. They were accident prone and unreliable. Very quickly the Postmaster General cancelled the mail contract which was the scheme's *raison d'être.* The Line failed with losses of £1.5m.

A sequence of bad luck and bad decisions followed. The giant steamships built in the 1860s for the London–New York line were simply too big for the passenger demand. The Line was closed in 1871. Then, there was the establishment of a new cotton mill in Carrick in the middle of a world shortage of raw cotton caused by the American Civil War. During the war, cotton exports from Portlaw had sunk to less than a quarter of what they had been. To ensure supplies Malcolmson's ships tried to run the North's blockade, and invested unproductively in Southern merchants. Then Joseph's widow Charlotte, perhaps sensing trouble ahead, decided to remove her substantial share of the capital. In 1866 a major bank went broke in

London, taking £2m of the Malcolmsons' money with them. Then, disgusted by this, another partner removed his £750,000 of capital. And in the meantime, the Malcolmson family were building for themselves lavish houses in Waterford, Clonmel, Dunmore East and Portlaw.

By 1870 things were so bad that William appealed to the Chancellor of the Exchequer and the Governor of the Bank of England for help, arguing that Malcolmsons were too big to be allowed to fail, with 2,900 workers in Portlaw and Waterford and 2,200 elsewhere in Ireland. They were refused.

Malcolmson Brothers finally declared themselves bankrupt in January 1877, less than twenty years after Joseph's death, with assets no more than one-third of liabilities.

'Shawlies' in Michael Street at the Peter's Street corner in front of Forristal's, a bakery and flour store. (Courtesy J. O' Neill collection)

The pig buyers' revolt—1897

The Ballybricken pig buyers were a formidable power in Waterford's commercial, social and political life in the late nineteenth century. They formed a different, more radical, elite compared to the generally unionist Quaker and Church of Ireland business people.

In the late nineteenth century there were four curing factories in the city—Francis Barnes of Summerhill, J. Matterson & Sons of The Glen, Henry Denny & Sons of Morgan Street, and J. J. Richardson, whose Queen's Bacon Factory was in Morgan Street. Between them they employed more than 800 people and supported 150 pig buyers. Tens of thousands of pigs were handled every month, flowing through the Ballybricken market via the pig buyers for export live or for processing by the factories.

The pig buyers were something of an oligarchy, a small number of large families very, if not fiercely, protective of their interests. In the 1880s these interests were under threat from competition from overseas, and restrictions imposed by the Germans on imports of pork products.

In 1884 they established the Pig Buyers Association and opened its impressive headquarters. Pride of place went to portraits of John Mitchel and Thomas Francis Meagher, the physical force rebels of the 1840s. This radical political alignment was contradicted later when they backed the constitutionally based Home Rule movement with considerable fervour. By 1892 the pig business was beginning to feel strong competition from Denmark, as the butter merchants had done before them. To cut costs, the factories moved to deal directly with farmers and cut out the middlemen, the pig buyers.

The pig buyers, hearkening back to Land League days, called for a boycott of the factories, and were prepared to enforce this. The Ballybricken men had gained a reputa-

Police escorting pigs to the slaughter house in defiance of the pig-buyers boycott. They have been transported by boat from southern Co. Waterford.
(Courtesy National Library of Ireland)

tion during the 1880s of supporting farmers, and simultaneously a reputation for being unafraid of violence. At one stage during the dispute rumours circulated about the pig buyers' plans to dynamite one of the factories, and no one doubted that they had firearms of various sorts.

Most farmers and the ordinary Waterford people backed the pig buyers. On one occasion the dockers refused to work a cargo of salt on the *Yarra Yarra* for Richardsons. Other dockers arrived from New Ross but they were 'persuaded' by their Waterford counterparts and the pig buyers to return home, which they did. Eventually Richardsons managed to hire labour in North Kilkenny and Laois and the *Yarra Yarra* was discharged and the cargo moved to the factory with RIC in attendance and batons drawn.

As the atmosphere grew tense, and the pig buyers

prepared to enforce their point of view, those farmers who chose to sell pigs to the factories needed police escorts as they brought their pigs through the city. The buyers then extended the boycott to publicans and eating houses that served the offending farmers. Finally the pig buyers put pressure on the men working in the factories, at one point a mob of 200 men attacking 15 Denny's salters as they went to Mass. Tempers were not improved when the bacon curers kindly offered to assist the emigration of the buyers and their families.

The dispute in its various phases would go on for five years, but at the end it was becoming clear that the factories were able to acquire enough pigs to keep going, and so the pig buyers accepted a compromise settlement.

John Redmond greatly added to his political capital when he successfully defended buyers accused of assault and disorder; this helped sustain active Ballybricken support behind the constitutional Home Rule movement.

Another scene from the pig-buyers boycott as police escort large herds from Tipperary and Kilkenny across the bridge.
(Courtesy National Library of Ireland)

Early motor cars on The Quay (Courtesy National Library of Ireland)

Motor cars in Waterford

The first motor car in Waterford was registered as WI1, and was owned by Herbert Goff, the son of a local businessman. To the astonishment of the local people he drove the Paris-built vehicle down The Quay in 1899.

Motoring did not catch on very fast in Waterford. By 1904 there were only 21 registrations, and a mere 45 in 1906. Waterford County, a separate registration code, had only 17 cars out of the 2,067 in the country as a whole in 1906.

Rather more advanced was the garage side, where Captain Bill Peare's Catherine Street works, opened in 1900 in conjunction with William Davis Goff, Herbert's father, is believed to have been the first commercial motor works in Ireland. Here Captain Peare assembled the first Irish motor-cycle, for Sir Hercules Langrishe. William Goff was an enthusiastic motorist, being founding Chairman of the Irish Automobile Club and a board member of Dunlop.

William Goff was a member of Waterford's group of Quaker and Church of Ireland businessmen. He was Chairman of the brewery Davis, Strangman, and at various times vice-chair of the Tramore Railway, a director of the Waterford Steamship Co., the Southern Steam Trawling Co., and a trustee of Waterford Savings Bank. He was a member of the Harbour Board and a director of the Waterford Chamber of Commerce. The Davis, Strangman brewery in Mary Street stood six storeys high, with malt houses, cask washing sheds and industrial shops. Goff was one of the city's largest employers.

The first run of the 7¼ mile Waterford and Tramore Railway was in September 1853, and this engine (No 1, later renumbered No 483) after several refits remained in service until 1935 when it was scrapped after being derailed at Carriglong bridge. The line was built by the famous Irish railway contractor William Dargan in only six months. Despite numerous plans down the years, the line was never connected to any other, so the ancient trains just trundled quietly to and fro on the single line between Manor Street station and Tramore. The journey took less than 20 minutes. (Courtesy J. O'Neill collection)

A Waterford saint—Little Nellie of God

Pope Pius X, later Saint, was very keen that children receive their First Communion as early as possible, as soon as they had reached the age of reason, i.e. seven years. This was a significant break with the previous custom which saw boys and girls making their First Communion in late adolescence and in a much less dramatic fashion. All the modern customs of special dresses, gifts of money and so on stem from this change initiated in 1910.

Nellie Organ, who was afterwards known as Little Nellie of Holy God, the Little Violet of the Holy Eucharist, was born the fourth child of William Organ who was a soldier based in the artillery barracks in Ballybricken.

Her mother instilled in her a great faith in 'Holy God' as she called him, but unfortunately died of tuberculosis when Nellie was not quite four years old.

Her father could not cope with looking after her and her sisters, so they were placed with the Good Shepherd Sisters at their industrial school in Sunday's Well, Cork.

In the convent Nellie greatly impressed the nuns with her pious ways and her devotion to 'Holy God'. So much so that they arranged for her to get the Bishop's special permission to receive her First Holy Communion at the unusual age of four and a half.

In the meantime, as well as caries of the jaw and a spinal injury, she had been diagnosed as having tuberculosis, like her mother. She was much on her own in bed, and spent the long hours 'talking to Holy God'. The Sisters were greatly impressed with her progress in religious knowledge and her devotion to the Eucharist. The doctor believed that she did not have long to live, and so it proved. She died in February 1908 only a few months after her First Communion.

Initially she was buried in the public cemetery of St Joseph where her grave became a shrine for the local people. After a year or so her body was transferred to the Convent Cemetery at Sunday's Well. Her body was reported quite whole except for the diseased jaw.

When told of this precocious child's life and death, Pius X declared that it had influenced him in the decision to make Confession and Communion available to seven-year-olds, a decision that enormously changed everyday Church practice.

Worries on the railway

It was bad news for Waterford when it was proposed that a new and rival port would be built at Rosslare, and another at Fishguard (1906). Looking for a shorter sea link with Wales, the Great Western Railway (GWR) had selected an unlikely location at Rosslare. Wexford harbour had silted up and Dunmore East had long since rejected a rail connection. Rosslare had a small pier but was not a natural harbour though it was protected from prevailing winds and that, apparently, was enough to secure its place in this massive Anglo-Irish investment.

The GWR had determined to take on their rivals on the Irish Sea, especially the London North Western's Holyhead route. Waterford worried about its existing steamer links with west Wales and the consolation of a rail link from the County Wexford port was no consolation at all, especially to those in shipping—including, of course, the Waterford Harbour Commissioners.

The legislation for the new ship/rail developments brought sweeping changes to the business of Irish Sea shipping and related rail services by amalgamations.

Naturally, Waterford sought to protect its interests. During negotiations a deputation from Waterford travelled to London and met Mr Nelson, Solicitor to the Great Western Railway. Nelson proved a difficult adversary and objected strongly to certain provisional clauses that had been agreed in Dublin, safeguarding Waterford's position.

After exhaustive debates Mr Nelson produced a memorandum with new clauses 'which he stated would be far more valuable for Waterford than the settlement which had been agreed to in Dublin.' This was said by the Harbour Board's legal adviser, Ernest Thornton, who was present at the discussions. Mr Thornton added: 'The members of the deputation now felt themselves to be in an extremely difficult and perplexing situation.' Time was pressing, and confusion had arisen on the worth of the Dublin agreement and, not unnaturally, on the clauses put forward by Mr Nelson. The Waterford men entertained the 'deepest suspicion' of the GWR's intentions. The deputation withdrew and resorted to their Parliamentary Agents (Holmes and Grieg).

Mr Thornton continued: 'Mr Grieg acted for us with great promptitude and within an hour we had the good fortune to be introduced by him to Sir Henry Oakley, General Manager of the Great Northern Railway, a gentleman of great experience and occupying the very highest position in the railway world.'

Sir Henry agreed to take home the Waterford papers. Next morning, to everyone's surprise, he took the Waterford side. His opinion was that the clauses proposed by Mr Nelson 'were worthless and could not be taken as intended bona fide to protect Waterford.' Sir Henry considered the Dublin agreement as being framed on the

A view of Sallypark in the 1890s, before the timber bridge was replaced

right lines and in the course of a later letter to Greg setting out his views in detail, he wrote: 'You must object as strenuously as possible to any attempt to limit the through booking to any particular route. The trade of the port must be free to go where it will and on fair terms. If these principles be steadily kept in view, the amalgamation will probably tend to the benefit and prosperity of the port.'

As a final note Sir Henry added: 'I am personally much obliged for the clear and intelligent assistance you have rendered me and I am sure your clients have been thoughtfully and carefully protected by your professional skill and experience.'

Armed with Sir Henry's advice the deputation returned to Paddington and resumed the discussion with new heart. Both sides now held firm. But after some weeks of argument the GWR finally agreed to the insertion of the 'Dublin' clauses only when Waterford 'in friendly but decided terms' pointed out that unless the agreed conditions were inserted in the Bill without further delay 'Waterford would actively oppose the Bill.'

This threat to collapse the whole deal, wrote Mr Thornton, had the desired effect.

Old Ferrybank

A royal occasion

On 2 May 1904 King Edward VII and his Queen Alexandra, briefly visited Waterford. The *Souvenir Programme* describing the visit is an elaborate presentation glorying in the full names and titles of all the participants. It has also portrait photographs of the King in full regalia, Councillor James A. Power, Mayor of Waterford and Alderman W. G. D. Goff. The Quay and Lismore Castle are well depicted but the show-stealers are stunning illustrations of the Imperial Hotel (now Tower Hotel) and Robertson, Ledlie, Ferguson & Co. (now Shaw's), festooned with bunting, garlands, drapes, and flags in the extravagant style of the age.

'Bobs', the famous British soldier (otherwise Field Marshal The Rt Hon. The Earl Roberts Bt VC KG KP GCB OM GCSI GCIE PC) was a member of one of Waterford's best known families.

Proceedings began with the arrival of the royal train at Waterford (North) at 12.50 pm, the Guard of Honour formed by the 1st Leinster Regiment with band and colour under the command of Major Canning.

In the port were the naval ships HMS *Melampus*, HMS *Curlew* and HMS *Skipjack*; they fired a royal salute on their Majesties' arrival. Rear Admiral Angus McLeod was also present and flew his flag in HMS *Aeolus*. Ships were dressed 'ship rainbow' fashion from 8 am to sunset, and were open to the public from 5 pm to 7 pm. After sunset the ships gave flash-light and search-light demonstrations.

Their Majesties were received at the station by the Duke and Duchess of Devonshire, the Marquis and Marchioness of Waterford and the Mayor. At least ten addresses of loyal welcome were presented—by the great and the good of the city (the Corporation, the Harbour Board, Federated Trades and Labour, Chamber of Commerce) and by various social and charitable organisations such as the United (Protestant) Dioceses of Cashel, Emly, Waterford and Lismore, the Young Women's Christian Association, the Young Men's Christian Association, the South-Eastern Provincial Grand Lodge of Freemasons, the Ladies of

Waterford citizens line the streets to greet King Edward VII and Queen Alexandra in 1904. (Courtesy J. O' Neill collection)

Waterford, and the Ancient Order of Foresters. The King considerately made a joint reply.

At 1.10 pm the royal procession, headed by Colonel Sir Neville Chamberlain, KCB, Inspector General of the Royal Irish Constabulary, proceeded along the Quays escorted by the South of Ireland Imperial Yeomanry, under Lieutenant L. L. Hewson. Luncheon was served in the Large Room, City Hall, catering was by the Imperial Hotel.

At 2.30 pm the royal party left City Hall, preceded by the Mayor in his carriage, accompanied by the Town Clerk. The procession went by Lombard Street and William Street to the Show Grounds, where they witnessed a show jumping competition at the Waterford Agricultural Society's Show.

At 3.45 pm the royal party left the Show Grounds for Waterford (South), leaving by train at 4.05 pm for Lismore to be guests of the Duke and Duchess of Devonshire. As was usual in such occasions, the Mayor, James Power, was knighted on the platform before the King mounted the train.

A DIVIL OF A GAME.

John Redmond, the leader of the Irish Parliamentary Party was MP for Waterford from 1891 until his death in 1918. As this Punch *cartoon shows, leading the Party was as difficult a balancing task as the new craze Diabolo.*

One of the ships that called in to Waterford on the occasion of King Edward's visit in 1904

Waterford's proud athletic tradition

The whole idea of sport has changed utterly since the early days of the *Munster Express*. There were traditional field sports, athletics and rowing on the Suir. Cricket had largely replaced hurling. Even Michael Cusack, soon to be the founder of the GAA, was an enthusiastic member of the French College (Blackrock) Cricket Club. Despite the rough roads and the unwieldy 'penny-farthing' bicycles, cycling was also popular, though it was definitely for young men only. Organised sport in specially set-aside

The hardy men of the Waterford Boat Club during their halcyon days in the early 1890s—their trophies proudly displayed.
(Courtesy National Library of Ireland)

grounds was hardly known. The first international Ireland v. England soccer match was not held until the 1880s, and then had to be played on the Leinster Cricket Club ground.

The first official Athletic Association to be formed in Ireland was the Irish Champions Athletic Club (ICAC) which ran from 1873 to 1884. This was an elitist association mainly centred around the colleges in Dublin. One of the main reasons why Michael Cusack formed the Gaelic Athletics Association (GAA) was to give all classes an opportunity to compete. However Cusack himself competed with the ICAC when he went to Dublin and in fact won the shot putt title in 1881.

As its name indicates, the GAA, as formed in 1884, had as its first priority the promotion of athletics. The first

All Ireland ever held were the Athletic Championships in Tramore at the Old Racecourse on the Back Strands in October 1885. At these championships Dan Fraher, a great nationalist from Sheheens (Fraher Field in Dungarvan is named after him), won the hop step and jump title, and Pat McGrath, from the Ballinamult area, won three medals.

In early 1885 another Athletic Association, called the IAAA, was formed and was affiliated to the British AAA. Athletic disunity has bedevilled the sport in Ireland for generations. There were many Waterford winners at these championships. Both associations continued to stage championships until 1923 when the NACA took over.

In the early years of the GAA championships, Waterford winners in the main were all field event athletes such as Tom Barry, Pat Keohan and James Wall, all from the Dungarvan area, and Pat McGrath from Ballinamult. Between them they won numerous Irish titles. The first Waterford athlete to win a track title was Davy Christopher from the Butlerstown area who won the GAA 880 yards in 1897. Between 1896 and 1912 Peter O'Connor and Percy Kirwan between them won many titles under both associations. Another fine champion of that era was sprinter J. J. Curry from the Rathgormack area. T. F. Flynn from Ballinamult was a mile champion and Dan Fraher's son Monnie was a jump champion as were Pat Power from Dungarvan and R. Power from Rathgormack.

Races at Duncannon, Co. Wexford along the River Suir, 1900 (Courtesy National Library of Ireland)

The Wild Man From Borneo

The Widger family were well-known horse breeders and dealers in the Waterford area. Tom Widger, the head of the family, supplied many horses to cavalry regiments throughout Europe. The youngest of his five sons was Joe, who was said to be 'a born horseman who could ride almost before he could walk'.

Widger's was a substantial business, supplying horses to the English, Dutch and Italian governments. It was said that two thousand horses a year passed through their hands. Various of the three or four hundred horses they kept on their 700-acre farm had run in races, but none had done better than 4th in the Grand National.

It was Joe's ambition to ride a winner of that race. At the age of fourteen he absconded from school and ran away to ride his first winner at Bangor. In 1893 he and his brother John bought a horse called The Wild Man from Borneo (named after two famous circus stuntmen) to ride in the Grand National. They entered him as soon as they could in the 1894 race. In the race The Wild Man From Borneo ran

Priests of St John's in the early 1900s (Courtesy National Library of Ireland)

the whole way with the leaders, and was one of the three that broke away from the field at the end. He took the lead at the second last fence, but in an exciting finish was narrowly beaten by the other two finishing fast.

After the race, Joe said that he did not realise how good the horse was and vowed to bring back him the following year, which he did. The weather leading up to the 1895 Grand National was not good and the ground for the great race was heavy. This year was to see one of the greatest Aintree racehorses, the magnificent Manifesto, make his debut, and as if this was not enough of a challenge, the 1892 winner Father O'Flynn was also at the starting gate.

During an uneventful race Joe kept The Wild Man near the rails just behind the leaders. At the last The Wild Man From Borneo was still in third place but after safely jumping the fence the horse was finally given his head and went past the two in front. The Wild Man from Borneo surged to the finish, although at the end was a mere one-and a half lengths ahead of the second horse. But that was enough—Joe had his longed-for achievement.

There was much celebration back in the Widgers' home and indeed throughout Waterford. Celebrations went on long and for many nights.

The Wild Man from Borneo came back to the Aintree course twice. He fell in 1896 and in 1897 he was pulled up. In that race he was racing under the colours of a Miss Norris, the first registered lady owner in the National. Miss Norris subsequently became Mrs Joe Widger.

Blessing of boats

Waterford's first Olympian

The first athlete associated with Waterford to compete in the Olympic Games was not a native of Waterford but he spent most of his life in the city and is regarded as a Waterford man.

Peter O'Connor (1872–1957) is regarded as one of the great long jumpers in Olympic history. He was a very nationally minded person who competed in the twilight of his great career in the special Olympic Games in Athens in 1906. He was then 34. He won the triple jump and finished second in his favourite event, the long jump. To his dying day he maintained that he was robbed in this event by a biased official. This official was actually the manager of the American team—and an American won the title.

Although O'Connor and other athletes had originally been given Irish uniforms, a change in the rules meant that only athletes nominated by National Olympic Committees (which Ireland did not have) could compete. This was one of a series of changes instituted in these Games that have become part of the Olympic tradition. For instance, there was a great increase in highlighting national origins, including the introductory march-in of the athletes behind national flags and the raising of the national flags during the presentation of medals. Despite a request to the Crown Prince George of Greece to intercede for him to be allowed to compete for Ireland his placings were awarded to the British. During the Games he and another Irish athlete, Con Leahy, climbed the pole and replaced the Union Jack flag with an Irish flag with the inscription 'Erin Go Bragh'—this was the current nationalist green flag with a harp, before the tricolour was adopted. The pole was guarded by Irish and American athletes. Ironically, the flag had originally, before the change in rules, been supplied by the British officials.

Peter O'Connor is still regarded as one of the finest long jumpers of all time. His jump of 24 feet 11 ¾ inches in Ballsbridge in Dublin in 1901 caused a sensation and set a new world record that lasted for over twenty years. It remained an Irish record for almost ninety years. He won six British long jump titles and two high jump titles as well as numerous Irish titles under both the rules of the GAA and IAAA. In 1900 the British had offered to pay full expenses to him to represent them at the Olympics but he refused and in so doing he more than likely sacrificed a gold medal as at that time he was in his prime as a long jumper. He was a judge at the 1936 Olympics.

What was exported from Waterford in 1906

In 1906 *The Irish Times* special correspondent visited Waterford. He devoted several paragraphs to a complaint about 'the antiquated toll system', on the bridge. It was, he felt, cutting Waterford off from the rest of the world. 'It would be difficult', he wrote, 'to estimate exactly the effect the toll system has on the trade of the city. The pinch must be considerably felt somewhere, when it is remembered that not a single cart-load could pass to and from the railway station on the opposite side of the Suir without payment.' (Somewhat surprisingly, neither he nor Michael McCarthy, who visited the city a few years earlier, refer to the bridge by the poetic name of 'Timbertoes'.)

Nonetheless, he was impressed by the export business Waterford was doing. The city, he wrote 'is of first importance, with its own line of steamers making direct for such centres as Liverpool, Bristol, Milford, Newhaven, Southampton, Dover, Plymouth and Glasgow besides several others.' He listed the exports in a single week in July. They were:

Cases of condensed milk	1064
Casks of ham	6
Bales of bacon	2092
Butter in various containers	13,645
Lard (hundredweights)	62
Pigs (live)	340
Cattle (live)	652
Sheep	1691
Horses	67
Cases of eggs	1225
Packages of poultry	197
Boxes of fish	178
Casks of porter	1241

'The Waterford people', he went on, 'will tell you that they have only one street and that is the Quay. Certainly the Quay is the principal street. Some of the shop-fronts on the Quay are calculated to grace any portion of Grafton Street . . . plate glass windows dazzling with the latest marvels in millinery and drapery.'

But what he was particularly impressed by, as a journalist, was the fact that Waterford actually supported an evening paper, the *Waterford Evening News* (as well as dailies and weeklies). Produced in three editions every day, the paper employed forty staff to produce it. It did not, of course, survive.

The heyday of Bonmahon Mines

In the early twentieth century a brave attempt was made to revive the copper mines of Bonmahon, on the Waterford coast.

There had been active copper mines in the Bonmahon area since the 1700s, and perhaps much earlier. Traces of copper were easy to see on the beach, and the famous authority Sir Robert Kane in his *Industrial Resources of Ireland* (1844) reported the local belief that many of the veins had originally been worked by ancient inhabitants of the area.

In its hey-day, in the middle of the nineteenth century, the mines were highly productive and profitable, with the ore fetching high prices from the smelters in Swansea, Wales. According to Sir Robert nearly 10,000 tons of copper were extracted in 1843, valued at £62,000.

Over 1,000 people worked in the mines at this time. Four or five steam engines pumped the water from the shafts, one of which was over 1000 feet deep. The ore was mined by hand, lifted by steam and then sorted for appearance and colour by a team of women.

The village of Bonmahon thrived, with shops and, so it is reported, 21 pubs. There were also two hotels, a pawnshop, a reading room and a small printing shop.

But gradually the best veins ran out, and by 1878 the mines were closed down, and most of the families emigrated to mine workings in the United States.

At the beginning of the twentieth century the Bonmahon Copper Mines company made an attempt to revive the old mines in the township of Knockmahon. The company was launched in 1906 with a capital of £200,000 and the blessing of the City of London. Initial reports were very positive, but within a year things turned sour. The attempt was not a success. But why?

The official reason given was that the coincidental flood of copper from mines in Africa and South America so depressed world prices that it was no longer profitable to work them. It is certainly true that world copper production rose by nearly 50 per cent between 1900 and 1906. Others looked deeper: questions were raised about the

The deserted workings of the Bonmahon mines (Courtesy National Library of Ireland)

competence and even honesty of the mining engineer; J. J. Walsh of the *Munster Express* believed that there had been a reluctance on the part of the British Government to allow Irish mines to thrive.

However that may be, the company ceased operations in 1907, and for a few years the workings were patrolled by a watchman. In 1911 this watchman was stood down, and locals began to loot the houses and machines, according to a police prosecution mounted in March 1912. One defendant was accused of stealing the materials of four separate houses, others a pumping machine, a roll-top desk and two safes. This was only a committal procedure, and some have wondered if the Bonmahon man drowned with the *Titanic* (which sank in April 1912) with an almost identical name to the house-stealer, was connected with this prosecution.

So the 'great hope' of 1906 and 1907 came to nothing, and although attempts have been floated since, the Bonmahon mines have remained a relic of past glories.

PART TWO
1911–60

'Timbertoes' replaced by a new bridge

The first bridge over the Suir at Waterford was built in 1794 by the American Lemuel Cox, using American oak. This timber bridge was supported by 40 sets of oaken piers, making navigation beyond it impossible. A few years after it was first built a drawbridge was created in the middle, a gap which was subsequently widened.

The bridge cost £14,000 to construct, plus £13,000 that had to be paid to the ferrymen to buy out their rights. To recoup this money, a toll was charged for anyone crossing the bridge. This was a source of continuing annoyance to Waterford people, especially once the railway station was established on the Ferrybank side. Jarveys (horse-drawn cabs) paid 6d each way to cross the bridge (which is why they did not wait by the station); pedestrians paid a halfpenny.

It was not until 1907, more than a hundred years after the bridge was first built, that the right to extract this toll was bought out by the corporation. It cost £63,000, of which £38,000 was provided by the government on the urging of local MP John Redmond. Since the cost of living actually declined during the nineteenth century, the original expenditure of £27,000, some of which had been provided by the government, had turned out to be a very good investment.

Soon a new bridge was needed. It was to be constructed of ferro-concrete by a Glasgow company. The new bridge was 700 feet long and 48 feet wide. The opening span was

The old wooden bridge being replaced in 1911 with the ferro-concrete John Redmond Bridge

80 feet. The total cost was £71, 000. The bridge was opened by John Redmond and was subsequently called 'The John Redmond Bridge'.

The Mayor, Michael Kirwan, members of the corporation and leading citizens met at 12 o'clock in the City Hall in preparation for going over to the station to meet Mr Redmond, who was travelling by train. The 1.30 pm train steamed in to the sound of exploding fog signals and cheers from the assembled thousands. Redmond proceeded down the Quays by carriage while an enormous procession formed behind. The cheering was continuous and greetings were waved from almost every window along the route. Several bands took part in the procession, including the Barrack Street Brass and Reed Band and the Thomas Francis Meagher Fife and Drum Band. At intervals the strains of 'A Nation Once Again' were taken up by the crowd.

Shortly before 3 o'clock Redmond, the Mayor, and the members of the Corporation drove in motor cars and carriages to the new bridge entrance and the opening ceremony took place. The Quay and its approaches were packed with an enthusiastic crowd of 25,000 spectators.

Not everyone agreed with the name 'Redmond Bridge'; the editorial in the *Munster Express* on 15 February read: 'We see no earthly reason why it should be described other than as 'the Waterford Bridge. . . if the river Suir were spanned by half a dozen bridges we could understand a particular bridge being singled out to differentiate it from the others. . . . We hope that no pawky sentimentalism will ever have it described officially as anything else.'

Construction in progress

Celebrating the erection of one of the piers

Horse-drawn traffic crossing the new bridge

Waterford's forgotten tragedy— the Battle of Le Pilly August 1914

by GORDON POWER

On the morning of 19 October 1914, 578 men answered the roll call of the 2nd Battalion Royal Irish Regiment. After fierce fighting in the battle of Le Pilly, only 290 men remained standing two days later. At least 38 of the men killed came from Waterford. It was said that after Le Pilly every street in the old city of Waterford received a War Office telegram informing them of the fate of a family member. The toll does not include the dozens of Waterford men who were wounded and captured, nor those who died afterwards of their wounds.

The 2nd Battalion Royal Irish Regiment landed in France on 14 August 1914, at the very beginning of the First World War. They fought in a number of bloody actions in north-east France over the next few weeks, including the battles of Mons, the Marne and La Bassée, as part of the 'race to the sea' as the German and British armies attempted to outflank each other. On the morning of 19 October the Royal Irish found themselves ordered to

Wounded soldiers in the First World War

capture the French village of Le Pilly. After an inaccurate British artillery barrage, the village was assaulted by the Royal Irish under the command of Major E. H. Daniell DSO. The attack proved to be successful and the German troops were pushed back from Le Pilly. Unfortunately, the French supporting attacks had not succeeded, and at dusk it became apparent that the position now held by the Royal Irish was very exposed.

The British battalions next to the Royal Irish were also stretched and early on the morning of the 20th they were compelled to withdraw because of heavy artillery fire, leaving the Royal Irish isolated and totally alone. This fact was not missed by the Germans who began a series of probing attacks and later very accurate artillery barrages. In the absence of new orders (brigade headquarters had withdrawn, neglecting to inform the Royal Irish) Major Daniell decided to await a British counter attack which would bring in fresh troops and support. But by 3 pm the situation was dire. The battalion had taken a lot of casualties (including the commanding officer) and it became necessary to take what ammunition remained from the dead and wounded and distribute it amongst the diminishing numbers of able-bodied troops. By about 5pm on the 20th the last remnants of the battalion were forced to abandon their brave stand and surrender.

Only 302 men were left alive of whom only about a hundred were still capable of walking. Some small groups of men, having run out of bullets, had fixed bayonets and charged the German positions trying to break out. A few men managed to break through and eventually make it back to British lines to report on the fate of the battalion. The rest, taken prisoner, faced four long years in prisoner of war and work camps. Many would die of disease, weakened due to poor food and living conditions. Others would carry the psychological or physical wounds for the rest of their lives. The village of Le Pilly was not rebuilt.

Royal Navy vessels rafted up on the Quays of Waterford during the First World War (Courtesy National Library of Ireland)

1918—a tightly fought election

John Redmond, the Parnellite and leader of the Irish Party, had been MP for Waterford since 1891 (when he defeated Michael Davitt for the seat), when he died of heart failure following an operation in March 1918. The First World War was in its fourth year, though with the Americans now involved, it was hoped to see the end of conflict.

In 1914, Redmond had believed (like most other people) that the war would be quick and short, and that it provided a chance for the Irish people to show their discipline and steadiness and so 'deserve' Home Rule. The Volunteer movement as a whole agreed with him, by fifteen to one. Redmond convinced many young Waterford men to enter the forces, which eventually led to many casualties.

His son Captain Willie Redmond stood in the subsequent by-election for his Westminster seat. He was

The French Church

challenged by Sinn Féin's Dr Vincent White of Broad Street, Waterford. The British forces in Waterford had many supporters; many had joined up for the war and there were numerous families dependent on war pensions and disability payments. There was also great loyalty to the Redmond name and the Home Rule campaign.

Although the war was coming to an end, the threat of conscription was still a big issue and various political heavyweights such as Arthur Griffith, the Sinn Féin leader, came to Waterford for a public rally and meeting. Joe McGrath, later of the Sweep and Waterford Crystal, was another.

Sinn Féin had a strategy to be at the polls and convince people on the day to vote for Dr White. Supporters had come from Clare and other parts of Ireland, some dressed as Volunteers. Captain Redmond wore his British army

The Walsh family (back row l–r) Clare, Edward (father), John, Fr Nicholas, Margaret, Willie (front row l–r) Margaret (mother) J. J., Pat
(Courtesy National Library of Ireland)

uniform so the stage was set for a confrontation. Dr White was assaulted by a Redmondite mob near Mount Sion, where voting was to take place.

The police were there too, some shots were fired in what was a very tense situation. Sports matches were cancelled to avoid clashes.

The result saw Willie Redmond win convincingly with 1,242 votes against 764 for Dr White. Redmond was one of the few Home Rule candidates outside Ulster to be elected in the subsequent general election. He took his seat in Westminster (not the Dáil) and was regularly re-elected, latterly as a Cumann na nGaedheal candidate until his death in 1932, aged 56. Dr White also sat for Cumann na nGaedheal between 1927 and 1932.

Sinn Féin supporters said *Beidh lá eile ag an bPaorach*.

Printing at the *Munster Express* 1920–60

By the 1920s, the *Munster Express* was automatically typeset in hot metal, by Linotype, the pages made up by hand on the 'stone' in large metal grids called formes. Line ads and half-tone pictures were produced inhouse, and metal plates made, which were fixed to wooden blocks exactly the height of the type. Printing was done on traditional Wharfedale flatbed sheet-fed machines. The paper was typically eight pages broadsheet, so two pages would be printed at once, the paper turned over and the reverse then printed. Once the whole paper was printed in this way, the sheets were folded, gathered and trimmed. A typical print run was 5,000 copies.

Printing the paper every week by no means filled the presses, so like other local newspapers the *Munster Express* ran a print jobbing business on the side. Ads extolling the virtues of good printing and advertising its jobbing printing skills appeared regularly on the front page. A regular house advertisement proclaimed: 'Important!!! The age we live in is one of Science, speed and progress. Those who fail to keep up with the times are left by the wayside'. 'We do everything' ran another ad: 'In Memoriam cards, visiting cards, a great variety of wedding cards as well as posters, programmes, billheads, memos, cloak-room tickets, card drive and raffle tickets, bookwork and catalogues of every description'. Much of this would have been too small for the Wharfedale, so proofing presses were used, including a venerable Columbia hand press.

Young Master Fitzgerald of Shortcourse, Waterford, proudly poses with his tricycle, 1920s (Annie Brophy collection)

The big innovation during the recession years of the 1930s was the introduction of news stories on to the front page, which had previously contained nothing but ads. This became a regular feature of the paper by the end of 1933. Another innovation was the purchase of a Linotype font of Gaelic type, the first regional newspaper in Ireland to take this step. Since the font was not used in the paper itself, this must have been to meet demand from the jobbing side. The period of the Second World War (1939–45), was even more difficult economically than the 1930s, but the young J. J. Walsh who, though his father was still alive, was effectively running the paper with his elder brother Patrick, was energetic in keeping the paper in production.

Taking seriously Seán Lemass's warnings about likely shortages (and perhaps remembering the problems caused by the German blockade in 1917) he foresaw the shortages of newsprint during the war period and built up large stocks of newsprint which he stored in a separate warehouse in Thomas Hill. This was a trumphant decision. Despite the ravages of the River Suir, which on one occasion flooded the newsprint store, the *Munster Express* had enough newsprint to last through the Emergency and help out other regional newspapers when they ran short. Printing the *Munster Express* during the Emergency was a swift job, since each weekly edition ran to just four pages.

The multiple magazine Linotype machine sent to the *Munster Express* was the last to arrive in Ireland until after the war. The ship bringing it to Ireland was bombed and the machine badly damaged. But T. C. Yelland, later to become chief engineer at the *Belfast Telegraph*, came down to Waterford from the North every weekend for some months until he eventually got the machine working.

In May 1945 ,as soon as the Second World War had ended, J. J. Walsh ordered a new Cossar press from Patrick Brothers, the Irish agents in Belfast; but post-war shortages meant that it wasn't commissioned until five years later. The years 1948 to 1950 saw the construction of a considerable extension to the *Munster Express* premises, to house its printing equipment, particularly the new Cossar. The great innovation of the new press was that it was printed from reels of paper, but from flatbed setting. Reel feeding of the paper was much quicker than sheet, and this enabled the *Munster Express* to meet the new circulation requirements of the 1950s and 1960s. The fact that the reel was printed from the flatbed made-up pages as before meant that there was no need to invest in a stereotyping department that in other systems created the 'flongs' that wrapped around cylinder-presses.

The new press was remarkable for its time, weighing 20 tons and capable of printing, folding and cutting several thousand copies of the newspaper an hour. During the 1950s, more innovations were installed, such as another multiple magazine Linotype, commissioned in 1953. In 1957, the paper was the first in the region to install electronic engraving for photographs. Printing capacity was again extended at the end of the 1950s.

On 13 March 1959, it was reported that John Elliott, a Waterford printer who had retired some years earlier, had died. He had started his career as a compositor (hand typesetter) with the old *Waterford Citizen*, then went on to work for other papers, including the *Munster Express*. He was among the last of the old Linotype men who were equally skilled at the even older tradition of hand typesetting.

By 1963, the *Munster Express* was advertising, as it had done in 1929, that it had the most modern equipment for commercial work, with the latest high speed presses ready to print the most complex, or simple, orders for companies large and small.

The Waterford Soviet

For three days in April 1920 the workers in Waterford controlled the city, creating what was called the 'Waterford Soviet'. This was a moment when the struggle for Irish independence was still fierce, and when the success of the Russian revolution had attracted world-wide attention.

The immediate occasion was news of a hunger strike by a hundred prisoners in Mountjoy Gaol, Dublin. On Monday 12 April a local railway union leader called Luke Larkin (no relation to Jim, who was at this time in Sing-Sing prison in the US on subversion charges), called a 24-hour general strike in protest. There was a big response the following day. As the *Munster Express* put it, 'all the shops were closed and the place was as quiet almost as a

Free State troops in the civil war

cemetery'. A procession formed in the Mall and marched up the Quay to the Cathedral where, despite the red flags and the red badges worn by many, the rosary was recited. (Foreign observers had noted with surprise similar religious activity during the Limerick Soviet of 1919.)

The Mayor, a Sinn Féiner, resigned in favour of Larkin and his associates, who were described as the Soviet Commissioners. They now controlled the city, issuing orders to be obeyed. A red flag was hoisted over the City Hall. The strike was enforced by pickets, who were not inclined to make exceptions. Lawyers and bank clerks who tried to ignore the workers' strike were forced away from their desks, and cinema owners were warned not to open.

Cars were stopped in the street by large gangs of picketers with sticks. In one case a police vehicle was nearly rolled into the Suir before it was learned that the occupants were escorting a lunatic to the nearest asylum. A wedding party from Fethard was given a permit.

Finally, on Wednesday 14 April a telegram was received from Dublin saying that the prisoners had been released. When this was confirmed the strike was called off. After another large procession, more speeches and thanksgiving prayers in the Cathedral, the Waterford Soviet, a fine piece of theatre, was over.

Waterford in the war of independence

Waterford city was quiet in the 1919–22 period, but the county was considerably more active. There was more action in west Waterford than in the east of the county.

The first casualty was in Baile na Gall near Ring when a policeman accidentally shot a local going into a pub. His name was Michael Walsh.

The IRA were badly in need of arms and some of the methods to secure them were brutal. Carrickbeg RIC barracks was attacked in May 1920 and partially destroyed. Other local barracks that were under-manned were closed in places like Clonea Power and Cappagh.

Not far away from Ring, in Piltown Dungarvan, a major ambush took place in November 1920. A lorry-load of troops from Youghal and some RIC men were caught in a trap after they came to help out while the Ardmore RIC barracks was attacked. The troops surrendered. The RIC men, who were acting as guides, were shot first and then the soldiers were also killed. The haul of arms taken was 26 rifles, 2 carbines, ammunition ands some bombs, plus some revolvers. A large monument now marks the location.

A less successful ambush took place near Tramore at Pickardstown, just before the town on the Waterford side. The plan was to attack the RIC barracks in Tramore and ambush a lorry-load of British troops expected out from Waterford to relieve the RIC men. The two lorry-loads of soldiers passed and were attacked by two sets of gunmen. But a shot was fired too early, which warned the troops in time to take the shelter of the railway bridge. The soldiers escaped with superior numbers against the East and West Waterford IRA brigades. Two volunteers, Michael McGrath and Thomas McGrath, of East Waterford were killed. (The Tramore GAA club carries the McGrath name in their honour.)

Another incident occurred at Kilmacthomas where a jury was disrupted before a trial in the court there. Another ambush took place at the Burgery near Dungarvan, where a Sergeant Hickey was captured and executed. The officer who carried out this raid was George Plunkett, brother of Joseph Plunkett, one of the executed signatories of the 1916 Proclamation. Plunkett railway station in Waterford was named after him in 1966.

The Strand Hotel in Abbeyside was burned by the Black and Tans, as well as three other houses.

A composite picture showing participants in the Troubles

An attempt was made to smuggle arms into Ring and Helvick from Germany, on a vessel called the *Frieda*, but the boat was diverted later to Cheekpoint on the Suir, where the arms cache was unloaded and then carried to Boatstrand pier.

Train derailments and other disruptions to traffic happened frequently. However, towards the middle of 1921 things calmed down and finally at the end of the year the Treaty talks got underway.

The Dublin GPO destroyed during the Rising

Killed in the Troubles 1919–23

- Paddy Cuddihy of Tramore, Patrick O'Reilly and Michael Fitzgerald of Youghal: sentenced to death by firing squad following a barracks attack.
- Michael McGrath of Poleberry, Waterford and Thomas O'Brien of Dunhill: killed in Pickardstown ambush, Tramore.
- John O'Rourke of Waterford: killed in a Butlerstown ambush.
- Maurice McGrath of Carrickbeg, Co. Waterford: died in July 1922, after an accidental shooting.
- John Dobbyn: similarly shot in the Comeraghs during the civil war in August 1922 after a comrade misused a gun.
- Thomas Kennedy of Rathgormack, Co. Waterford: died in the Glen of Aherlow in 1922.
- John Doyle of Waterford: killed in July 1922, after the civil war siege of the Four Courts in Dublin.
- Thomas Walsh of Waterford: shot by Free State troops in February 1922.
- Michael Moloney of Waterford: shot after a raid in February of that year.
- Andrew Power of Great Island, Waterford: died in Kilkenny gaol 1923.
- John Walsh of Kilmacthomas: suffered a similar fate in Kilkenny.

There were more casualties in South Kilkenny, with the villages of Mooncoin , Kilmacow and Hugginstown being noted for their rebel activity.

Munster Express office occupied in the Civil War

After the Treaty was signed in December 1921, and accepted by a majority of the Irish Cabinet, everyone was pleased to see the Black and Tans as well as the Auxiliaries off the streets. With the positive (if narrow) Dáil vote for the Treaty, there was hope that peace could return, But Republicans were not happy and after failing to persuade the people of their views in the general election in June, they brought out the guns again in the cause of what they described as 'unfinished business'.

Armed men, known as the Irregulars, began to seize power around the country as the British troops had left. Facing them was the official Free State army—often recent comrades of the Irregulars they were now squaring up to. Immediately, a Free State contingent marched south from Dublin to take back control of Waterford and other towns and cities from the Republicans.

The Republicans, led by Pax Whelan, who had been very active in the War of Independence, quickly occupied all the main buildings in Waterford, including the gaol and barracks in Ballybricken, the GPO and Clyde Shipping premises.

They also occupied the *Munster Express* premises. Irregulars from Dunhill and Fenor arrived a day before the Free State troops attacked. Inside the printing works family and workers remained on the premises and worked normally as the rebel occupiers prepared defences. Nontheless the newspaper's position, between the rebels in the gaol and the Free State troops on Misery Hill with their 16-pounder, was not comfortable.

The staff included Michael Ryan, the typographical trade union official who had been caught up in Dublin during Easter 1916. They continued composing and typing even though shell fire was audible going overhead towards the barracks. Some staff compared the noise to what they had heard in London during the Great War, when the German Zeppelins crashed there.

Eventually, one of the rebels, James Carroll, started firing from the upstairs window across the river to the incoming Free State army. Then things changed. Fire was quickly returned, and it began to get dangerous. A man was killed in Hanover Street.

Mass was said by Father Nicholas Walsh, a son of the Editor home from Glasgow. Captain Power of the rebels ordered all to leave who were not fighting. Staff and family then agreed it was too risky to stay. Many families had gone to Tramore, but there was a fear of looting so the Walsh family went to a house in Bolton Street owned by David Hyland, a former city sheriff.

Finally, a detachment of Irregulars told the family to leave since they were taking over buildings on the Quay to defend Waterford against the Free State troops coming from the Leinster side. The bridge had been lifted but eventually the troops crossed the river from Ferrybank.

The Free State army had artillery given to them by the departing British army, thus were much better armed and trained. The Free State artillery silenced the rebel guns in Waterford at the gaol and barracks where machine gunners put up much resistance. The barracks was set on fire.

The rebel occupiers were named as follows in the *Munster Express* centenary edition (1959): James Carroll of Griffith Place, Mulie Fanning, John E. Myler of Clyde Shipping, Miss Molly Morrissey (later Mrs Haberlin of Ferrybank) who acted as a Red Cross nurse.

Their weapons included a Webley revolver and some small pistols—but no machine guns or rifles—which were of little use firing across the river. Consequently the Irregulars could only maintain a weak defence of

Waterford, so after two to three days the occupation was over. As Pearse and the Volunteers had discovered in 1916, it was a cardinal error in tactics for a weaker force to allow itself to be drawn into a siege situation. As a memento, there are still some bullet holes visible in the old reporters' office of the *Munster Express*.

Many years later, for the 1959 Centenary edition of the *Munster Express*, a great story was written on the invasion and battle for Waterford—'Now it can be told' as the headline put it.

With the Waterford battle over after a few days fighting, the Irregulars retreated to the West and Kilmacthomas. General Prout with the Free State forces headed to Carrick and South Tipperary to relieve the Suir valley towns.

Staff were back at work on Monday in time to publish the regular edition on the Thursday. No daily papers were available so there was huge interest in the county and city in the story on the siege. Later, J. J. Walsh (who was sixteen at the time) told how he and a brother brought papers by bicycle to Mooncoin then on to Piltown across supposed enemy lines and into Republican-occupied Carrick. The load was lightened after earlier parcel drops in Mooncoin and Fiddown.

They had a permit to travel from General Prout and Colonel Heaslip; the permit worked well in the Free State controlled area, but was of little use beyond that. They travelled across fields, stumbling over trenches and trees put down to block the Free State advance. They carefully did not tell Republican sentries that they were carrying newspapers with the full story of the fall of Waterford, which would have been bad for morale. The papers would have been destroyed and they would have been arrested. They were lucky not to be searched.

The *Munster Express* had missed a week's publishing, due to the division of the area and war. Paper was rationed at the time so there were only six pages in the edition on the siege. On the way back they called on the local correspondent, Seán O Floinn, having kept him a paper; he advised them of a safe route home.

The Waterford Redmond Bridge was not blown up during the Rebel attack, but elsewhere there was serious damage done.

Rail line bridges were destroyed across the south of the country to disrupt communications and movement of troops. The beautful Ballyfoyle/Stradbally viaduct was blown up as was the road bridge along the Tramore to Dungarvan coast road to safeguard Dungarvan against the Free Staters. Dungarvan fell on 23 August.

Erskine Childers was found near Fiddown and shot. He had brought the guns to Howth for the Easter rising but his last days were by the Suir as he tried to escape capture.

Republicans and de Valera went to hide in the Knockmealdown Mountains.

The Carrickshock Memorial

The Carrickshock Memorial was dedicated in April 1925. It commemorated an event of more than 90 years before, an incident in the Tithe War. Three local men, James Treacy, Patrick Power and James Phelan were killed in an attempt to snatch a hated process-server from a large contingent of police. The Memorial describes the 'ever-memorable and decisive tithe fight' in which 'they and their ever-faithful comrade heroes' suffered and died.

The Carrickshock Memorial

In December 1831 40 police were escorting the process-server Edward Butler about his law business, when they were accosted by a crowd of several hundreds. The crowd had been summoned by the ringing of a local chapel bell (by whom is still unknown). They demanded that the police give up the process-server. They refused. James Treacy, the son of a prosperous local farmer, lunged into the packed ranks of the police in an attempt to extract him. He was violently repulsed, and subsequently died.

The infuriated crowd then began to rain large stones on to the police from the high walls on either side of the boreen. Pitchforks, hurling sticks and clubs were also used. The police were so tightly crushed into the lane that they were unable to fire properly in retaliation or even reload. Eventually, Butler, thirteen police and two other farmers were also dead.

The event remained prominent in local memory, being interpreted according to the needs of the day. At the opening of the Memorial, Edward Walsh of the *Munster Express* declared exuberantly that when the people of Hugginstown crushed the Crown forces in 1831, 'they turned the tide and marked not alone an epoch in the history of this country but that of the civilised world (cheers)'.

Ten years later, in September 1934 at the height of the Economic War, the *Munster Express* reported that a gathering of Blueshirts in Hugginstown were told how the men of Carrickshock had resisted British tyranny in 1831, and they were not going to allow 'a so-called native government' to impose a similar tyranny.

In 1953, the Memorial was repaired, and J. J. Walsh of the *Munster Express* (being given, as his paper recorded, a rousing reception) used the occasion to remind the crowd that despite emigration Ireland was a country worth fighting for, and working for.

By the 175th anniversary in 2006, the Carrickshock Memorial Committee preferred to think of the event as 'a stand against injustice' and a 'fight for their rights' by the 'men and women' of the day. It also acted as a marker and a rallying point for the local community.

Edward Walsh and his daughters. Clare (on the left) worked on the administrative side of the Munster Express *before becoming a Cistercian nun. She was one of the foundresses of St Mary's Abbey in 1932, the first Cistercian monastery for contemplative nuns in Ireland since the Reformation. Margaret (on the right) also worked on the administrative side of the paper.*

A De La Salle hurling team in different county hurling strips 1933–4 (Annie Brophy collection)

Gaule's pick-up truck on Lombard Street (Annie Brophy collection)

Munster Express proprietor becomes Mayor of Waterford

In July 1928 the *Munster Express* reported that its Editor and proprietor Edward Walsh had been elevated to the Mayoralty of Waterford. He had first joined the Council in 1901, when, after a hard-fought battle, he became the youngest member.

In a full public career since then he became Chairman of the Board of Guardians (looking after the poorhouse), and a leading proponent of the movement to abolish the tolls on the old bridge.

In 1915 he was High Sheriff of the City, and in that capacity took the chair at meetings of the Mental Hospital Committee; he was for long Chairman of the Sanitary Authority and the Holy Ghost hospital. He was a leading member of numerous Catholic organisations such as the St Vincent de Paul and the Cathedral Confraternity.

In politics Edward Walsh was a longtime support of John Redmond, as the *Munster Express'* unenthusiastic reporting of the 1916 Rising—under the heading 'The Outbreak in Ireland'—made clear. On the other hand, he was an active promoter of the Carrickshock Memorial, recording an incident in the Tithe War, finally erected in 1925.

Edward Walsh died in 1946, aged eighty-three, a few years after he had handed over control of his newspaper to his sons Patrick and Joe (J. J.).

Waterford industries 1920s–1950s

In the period after Independence Waterford widened its economy and mustered a wide range of manufacturing activities, benefitting particularly from the new legislation of the early 1930s designed to protect Irish industry.

But Waterford had always been a working city. Bacon curing and brewing had been staple industries and Denny's had a lineage in bacon curing going back to 1820. In the 1930s there were two factories processing over a thousand pigs a week. Meat processing also had another great name, Clover Meats, deriving from the co-operative movement. Not far from the city had been the great pioneering operation of Malcolmson's of Portlaw, with its enormous cotton and shipbuilding empires.

Brewing had a reputation in the city going back even further. Davis, Strangman & Co. dated from 1792 and the tradition was picked up by Cherry's and in the 1950s Phoenix Ale was developed to a prize-winning standard.

Goulding Fertilizers had nineteenth-century roots starting in 1878 at Gracedieu and in 1802 they moved to a riverside location at Newrath.

The north side of the river was more suited to port related industries and was bordered by the railway. It was also home to other farm related businesses in grain and flour milling. Three companies worked side by side, R. & H. Hall, grain, Flake Maize, and Waterford Flour Mills. The buildings associated with these activities remain some of the most prominent city landmarks. The grain trade brought some of the finest and largest ships to the port from as far away as Australia, South America, the Gulf of Mexico and the Great Lakes.

A very significant development in 1937 was J. & L. F. Goodbody's jute spinning and weaving factory at Tycor. At its peak 500 were employed and the plant fitted comfortably in a block of its own surrounded by a well-organised 1930s urban housing development set on a considerable rise above the old city. A related activity also in the jute sector was the Waterford Sack & Bag Company which started in 1933 and employed up to 150 at its premises in Anne Street and Grattan Quay.

Waterford Ironfounders was another enterprise of the 1930s. Incorporated in 1936 as Allied Ironfounders (Ireland) Ltd, an associate of the British group of that name, it became independent in 1952 and by 1955 was a subsidiary of the Masser Group. Up to 300 employees were engaged at the 11-acre Bilberry foundry manufacturing cookers, heaters and stoves—including famous brand names such as Rayburn and. Stanley. The foundry occupied the site of the former Waterford South rail station and enjoyed a rail link with the national network for many years.

Waterford Metal was a post-war investment and in 1949 it opened at Gracedieu producing a wide range of metal products and also engaged in sheet metal engineering. It eventually employed up to 100 people.

The National Board & Paper Mills manufactured a wide range of paperboard used for the production of fibreboard and corrugated containers, cartons and boxes and also served the building industry. On a 35-acre site at Granagh the factory had a massive floor area of 8½ acres and employed 400 during the 1960s and 70s.

The range of business activity in Waterford before and after the Second World War was impressive for a small city. Among them was ACEC, a subsidiary of a Belgian company, manufacturing electric transformers and employing 210. It was also based at Tycor. Smaller but significant employers were Tyresoles (tyre re-treading), Power Seeds (seed and nursery goods), Irish Radium Products (polishes and leather dressings), Hearne & Co., cabinet makers and specialising in church and school furniture. There was also Waterford Products (inks and shoe polish), Waterford Sack & Bag, Waterford Brick & Tile and Waterford Electrical.

Taking up the running and at peak employing as many as 3,000 people was Waterford Crystal—altogether another story.

The boot factory, Waterford, 1941. Courtesy Fr. Browne S. J. Collection

The Stradbally Mystery, or
The case of the missing postman

Having done his rounds on Christmas Day 1930 (he looked after the Stradbally–Kilmacthomas route), postman Laurence Griffin stopped off at Whelan's Hotel, Stradbally for a drink. Next morning his bicycle was found on the road, undamaged, and he had apparently disappeared into thin air. Griffin, who was a married man with a young family, was never seen again.

Extensive searches were initiated in the then modest glare of national publicity. Bogs, fields, quarries and graveyards were all scoured. Anonymous letters suggested certain clifftops, or a particular orchard. Eventually the Guards began to think that the missing postman had probably been tipped down one of the disused mine shafts of the old copper mines of Bonmahon. The deepest of these, in Tankardstown, was reputed to be over 1,400 feet deep and full of water. Another shaft, much less deep, was explored by an English diver. Elaborate structures were built over the mines to enable explorations, including the use of grappling hooks, watched by an attentive crowd brought by enterprising local bus proprietors. Nothing was recovered.

In the meantime, ten people were arrested and accused of Larry Griffin's murder (and of stealing his official cap, value £5). These were the proprietor of the hotel where he had taken his drink, his wife, son and daughter, a couple of farmers, a National School teacher, a labourer and two Guards. They had all been in the hotel that day. They denied having anything to do with it, and it was hard to prove anything before the poor man's body was found.

The *Munster Express* reported that some people in Stradbally claimed he was not dead at all, but had merely absconded.

The Guards found it difficult to get any information about the case. Indeed a judge later complained bitterly that the people of Stradbally had 'closed up like an oyster'. With disgraceful lack of public spirit, in order to protect someone, he supposed, the neighbours 'closed their mouths and refused to give the police any assistance'.

Griffin's body was never found. Whenever any remains were discovered throughout the 1930s the cry was raised 'is this the missing postman?' But it never was.

The ten accused were released, and the hoteliers successfully sued the *Waterford News* for a circumstantial account of Griffin's last hours. According to the paper Griffin had accused one of the people in the bar of stealing some money he had dropped. 'Griffin's manner was none too mild' the reporter wrote; a fight broke out and Griffin fell heavily against an iron stove, tearing a long gaping wound in his temple and eventually dying there. In some panic, so the story went, the body was wrapped in a blanket and with a 56 lb weight attached to the feet sunk to the bottom of Ballinasisla mine shaft.

The Dublin jury agreed that this was an outrageous libel, and awarded the plaintiffs £1700 in damages— enough to buy a 50-acre farm.

So the story of the missing postman is still a mystery.

Blueshirt rally in Carrick to protest against the Economic War

On 1 June 1934 the *Munster Express* reported that 'General O'Duffy was met on the Dublin Road outside the town of Carrick-on-Suir by 6,000 Blue Shirts and about 800 women and girls wearing blue blouses. One hundred horsemen headed the procession and 26 men each 6 feet high formed a bodyguard. It was estimated that between 8,000 and

10,000 people were in the vicinity of the platform.'

The opposition politics of the time were confused. Fianna Fáil had been in power for two years, but because of their aggressive radicalism—'a slightly constitutional party' as Lemass famously called them—they aroused opposition among conservative Catholic voters, and those who stood for a traditional trading relationship with the British Empire, preferably inside the Commonwealth. The *Munster Express,* conscious of Waterford's trading interests, was inclined that way.

These elements had combined together as the United Ireland Party (UIP, now more usually called Fine Gael, but the English name was then more widely used). Heading this party, for the moment, was the erratic General O'Duffy. He was also the leader of the Blue Shirts, a grouping that had begun in 1932 as the Army Comrades Association and now was on its fourth name as the League of Youth. In September 1934 he was forced out of the United Ireland Party by more politically astute colleagues.

The UIP's main cause of contention was the devastation caused by the Economic War. By refusing to pay the land annuities, de Valera stimulated retaliation by the British, specifically with punitive tariffs on agricultural products. Waterford's farmers were badly hit. The fishermen of Tramore and Dunmore were equally affected. Waterford's pig trade was also hit.

The sitting Fine Gael TD Mrs Redmond, widow of John Redmond's son Willie, told the audience that the UIP stood for prosperity for Ireland's farmers, and that it was sheer humbug to call the farmers' best customer a foreigner and our ancient enemy and to pretend that the loss of the British market was a good thing for Ireland. Farmers were fast going down financially and the country was becoming bankrupt as a consequence. A businesslike and decent government would have long ago settled the Economic War.

Mrs Redmond retained her seat until her death in 1952. Fianna Fáil held two out of four seats in Waterford for thirty years, between 1927 and 1957.

TELEPHONE Nº 189.
TELEGRAMS :- "WALSH, AUCTIONEERS"

Established 1849.

BANKERS—THE NATIONAL BANK.

Thomas Walsh & Son

Auctioneers and Valuers,
House, Land, Insurance and General Agents,
COMMISSIONERS FOR AFFIDAVITS.

Offices and Antique Furniture Warerooms :
THE MALL, WATERFORD

Valuations for Probate and other purposes made.
Auctions of Furniture, Cattle and Farm Effects, personally conducted.
House Property and Land Valued and Sold by Auction.

Peter O'Connor from Parnell Street (standing third from right) with his comrades in Spain. Between 1936 and 1939 fourteen young Waterford men volunteered to fight with Franco and eleven (including O'Connor) to fight against him. Four of the latter were killed.

The Spanish Civil War

The vast majority of the Irish people, including J. J. Walsh of the *Munster Express*, believed that Franco and his armies were on the side of God in the great Civil War that broke out in Spain in July 1936.

Propaganda by and on behalf of the Catholic Church repeatedly proclaimed: 'the Church is in danger!' Vivid stories of the murder of priests and nuns, the looting of churches and monasteries, and the stealing of clerical goods were proclaimed from pulpit and lecture hall to rapt audiences. For the faithful what was happening in

Spain (and in Russia and Mexico) was all part of 'SATAN'S TERRIBLE ANTI-GOD CAMPAIGN', as an *Irish Independent* headline put it.

The stories were covered at length in the *Munster Express*. In August 1936, barely a month after the outbreak of the war, for instance, a headline proclaimed 'IRISH NUN'S THRILLING ACCOUNT OF SPAIN'. Sister Mary Bridget Kehoe, who was staying with her sister in Barronstrand Street, told of 'Reds' setting fire to churches, evicting nuns and orphans into the street and the brutal shooting of priests. Although she personally had not witnessed such things (indeed her own convent was 'comparatively quiet') she knew well that 'hundreds and thousands of priests were being done to death in this callous fashion day after day'.

Fired up by these accounts, in December 1936 12 young Carrick men left the town to join the Irish Brigade in Spain (led by the Blueshirt General O'Duffy) to fight with Franco. They travelled by rail to Galway where they joined a steamer called the *Dun Aenghus* where 600 other men were en route for Spain. The Carrick men were seen as having future careers for their valour in 'fighting Bolshevism which is now threatening unhappy Spain.'

Their names were: Joseph Gilman, Thomas Kearney, New Street; J. Darmody and E. and J. O'Neill, Ballyrichard Road; W. Burke, Long Lane; J. Holloway, Level Street; J. O Gorman, Town Wall; M. Nugent, John Street; J. McCarthy, Carrickbeg; J. Russell, Greenside and J. Meets, Town Wall.

Information on the war was poor at the time but the *Munster Express* did get sight of a letter from General Franco. In the edition of 8 October 1937, a letter from the General, on behalf of the Spanish people thanking a member of the Irish Brigade from Carrick on Suir, T. F. Kearney of Irish Brigade 135 B Company, for his efforts, was published in the 'Carrick Notes'.

But there were volunteers from Waterford on the Republican side as well. In fact out of 11 Republican volunteers, 4 were killed. Two brothers Power from Ballytruckle and working in Waterpark were killed. Jackie Lemon of Greyfriars was another fatality as was Jackie Quinlan of South Parade. George Browne of Inistioge, Co. Kilkenny was also killed. Peter O'Connor of Parnell Street was another participant. A Waterford teacher called Frank Edwards, who had previously been sacked from Mount Sion for his left-wing views and was a doyen of the Left in Waterford, was one of the participants on the Republican side. On his return he found it hard to secure work in Catholic schools. J. J. Walsh recalled how this able teacher had to leave for Dublin and eventually teach in a Jewish school in Dublin.

Many fought with the Basques and Catalans along with the English in the International Brigade in Northern Spain. Ironically, some of the Brigade were ex-Black and Tans but the Irish fought with them.

On their return, opponents of Franco were often ostracised and found it hard to get employment as they were deemed Communists. They were even refused Communion in churches.

Many years later, J. J. Walsh, by then sole Editor of the *Munster Express*, made a point of going to Spain to attend the funeral of General Franco in 1975.

Gaol Wall disaster monument at Ballybricken, Waterford

The saddest Waterford casualties of 'The Emergency' were undoubtedly the nine people killed when the great wall of Ballybricken Gaol collapsed in the early hours of the morning of 4 March 1943 and crushed some small houses in King's Terrace.

They were directly casualties of the time because the 40-foot wall, which towered only 8 feet from the houses, collapsed as a result of a clamp of 120 tons of wet turf laid against it. Not only did the turf (part of Waterford's response to the shortage of imported coal) press its weight against the wall itself, but at the same time moisture undermined the wall's foundations. As much as 300 tons of turf and masonry fell onto the row of houses. Not much thought seems to have been given to the possible consequences of putting the turf there.

A particularly awful feature of the incident was that the victims ranged in age from just two-and-a-half to 60 years of age. Seven of the nine people who died were under 20.

Local residents, mostly still in bed, were left trapped under fallen masonry and wet turf. Rescue services were supported in the recovery effort by revellers who had been attending the Beagle Ball at the Olympia Ballroom. Residents of surviving houses on King's Terrace were evacuated after the disaster and cared for over a three-week period by the Red Cross at St Joseph's Boys Club on the Yellow Road.

More than 60 years later, members of Waterford City Council unanimously agreed in September 2004 that a site should be provided for a monument commemorating the nine people killed in the Gaol Wall disaster. Designed by Co. Wexford artist Declan Breen who was also responsible for the sculpture and water feature at the main entrance to Waterford Regional Hospital, the new memorial is sited near the Bull Post on the green area at Ballybricken. The installation on a platform features a bronze plaque with the names of the nine victims laid horizontally on the raised ground with a large bronze ivy leaf also fixed to the ground.

The Ballybricken Gaol Wall disaster—nine people were crushed to death as the turf cascaded on to their houses while they were in bed. Seventeen others were injured (Annie Brophy collection)

Exporting horses to England during the Emergency (Annie Brophy collection)

Ireland stayed neutral in the Emergency 1939–45

The 1939 announcement of war coincided with the Cork–Kilkenny All Ireland final in Dublin, where future Taoiseach Jack Lynch was to play. A number of south Kilkenny readers of the *Munster Express* made it to the final.

Faced with a worsening international situation, *Munster Express* proprietor J. J. Walsh took Seán Lemass's 1938 advice seriously, and stocked up on newsprint. People could see that Hitler's invasions of Austria and Czechoslovakia, on the grounds of protecting German minorities, were not good signs. In fact J. J.'s prudent decision meant that there was never a paper problem during the Emergency period for the *Munster Express*, and indeed it was able to supply rival publications.

As shortages began to bite, trains in Ireland were later to be fuelled by turf and the journey to Dublin could take four hours, but at least there were trains still operational.

J. J. Walsh recalled of those times when he was single and had just taken over the editing of the paper that he had the time of his life. He could leave the office early in summer, get a train to Tramore and get in a game of golf.

Advertising was slack, papers were limited to 6–8 pages by the Minister for Supplies Seán Lemass (later Taoiseach). Staff in the *Munster Express*, like many at the time, were on reduced working hours.

Imported goods such as coal, petrol, jam, white flour, tea and cigarettes were very restricted, so J. J. could not drive a car—nor could anyone else, except gardaí, clergy or doctors, by Government order. Cycling was the way to get around and walking was very popular. On the other hand, there was no shortage of basic foodstuffs, though

Cattle hides bound for the Irish Leathers tanning factory in Portlaw (Courtesy Annie Brophy Collection)

slum dwellers in Dublin, whose basic diet had been white bread and jam, suffered badly. In the country, people had enough to eat compared to Britain and Europe. Some got rich trading in the black market for tea, tobacco and other luxuries such as wine.

Work was short, so many went to work in English factories; women left too, including J. J. Walsh's future wife Josephine who nursed in England in the naval hospital in Greenwich, London. Her sister Mai was bombed and evacuated twice in the blitz at the same hospital. Many also joined the forces, some were killed, others captured like a prominent local doctor, who was held by the Japanese and still managed to live a long, healthy and prosperous life afterwards. However, there were nothing like the fatalities of the First World War.

Those who wanted to join up took the train to Belfast, others were in the American or Canadian forces. Fifty thousand Irish joined up. Going in the opposite direction, many Irish living in England brought children to live with grandparents in the war to avoid the blitz. Writers in the 1920s and 1930s had exaggerated the likely effects of aerial bombardment, so many people believed that it would be easy for the Germans to crush London. The bombing of Dresden and other cities later showed that it could be done, but not without overwhelming force.

Ireland stayed neutral with huge public support for the de Valera stance, despite the hectoring and criticism of Churchill, who wanted ports back from Cork, Kerry and Donegal. A German invasion was planned in 1940 if the aerial Battle of Britain had been successful. They could have taken Ireland in a week, despite the efforts of the Local Defence Force.

War-time reports in the *Munster Express,* as in other papers, were subject to censorship, with scrupulous avoidance of anything that might give comfort to either side; this made the reportage that we have today difficult. In particular, the Irish people did not learn until after the war of the concentration camps.

Ireland came out of the war better than most, Irish farmers did well from higher food prices, as they had done in the the Napoleonic wars and in the First World War. Trade was slow afterwards. At the end of the war Operation Shamrock settled German orphan children in Ireland including in Waterford and Kilkenny.

The young managers of Turf Importers Ltd (Annie Brophy collection)

The windows of Sage's furniture shop 1940s (Annie Brophy collection)

Building the Rex Cinema in Tramore 1945 (Courtesy Annie Brophy Collection)

Bombs and planes during the Emergency

Although the war between Britain and Germany was not supposed to involve neutral Ireland, inevitably it did. A few German planes went off course and did damage. One bombed the Shelburne Co-op in the Campile, Co. Wexford, an area where there were keen readers of the *Munster Express*. Five bombs were dropped destroying the creamery and other buildings. Several people were killed. This was on 26 August 1940. Taoiseach de Valera complained to the German embassy about the attack. Some said it was a warning to the Irish government to be careful about supplying food to Britain, its major trading partner.

On 23 August 1942 a German Luftwaffe plane crash-landed in Carriglong near the Tramore–Waterford road having being shot down by a Spitfire after returning from a reconnaissance mission of Belfast. The actual location was on Owen Power's farm, where a major fire ensued. The air dogfight between the twin engine German Junkers bomber aircraft and the Spitfire could be seen from the Promenade in Tramore. The victorious British Spitfire did a loop of celebration after downing the German plane, whose engine had gone on fire. The crew survived and were brought to the military barracks in Waterford and then on to the Curragh for internment during the war.

At night German bombers could often be heard flying up the Irish coastline before going right across the Irish

Sea to hit cities such as Cardiff, Bristol, Liverpool and Manchester. There was a blackout in Waterford, but people watched along the Quays, as the bombers brought their deadly cargo up the Irish Sea.

British aircraft also made emergency landings when they ran out of fuel. Halley's farm in Crobally saw a Polish pilot land an RAF plane in April in 1941. The plane was a light bomber that was based in Stranraer, Scotland.

Another RAF plane went down in Ballybrack, Kilmacthomas, coming from Pembroke, Wales. The pilot was short of fuel and brought down his Hurricane so carefully that it was later put back into service by the Irish Air Corps, after a deal with the RAF in 1943.

Ballybeg in Waterford also saw a crash landing near the city in 1943. The RAF Wellington had to do an emergency landing after losing fuel. The four crew were brought into custody, then on to the Curragh. Locals took many souvenirs from the plane, much to the annoyance of the military authorities who were slow getting there.

Irish ships bringing much needed supplies were hit by German torpedoes or mines. Many mines landed on Irish shores, some exploding. Some Irish ships that traded with Waterford were destroyed in the war such as the *Irish Pine*. Mines littered the Irish coast. One was found on Tramore beach and brought up by trailer to a garage on Queen Street, where a careless mechanic tried to disarm it with a hammer. In the end he blew it up along with the old Cheasty garage. A man called Fitzgerald was killed and others were injured.

First sod of new glass factory turned

In late March 1947 the first sod of the new Waterford Glass factory at Ballytruckle was turned by the Mayor, Councillor Coffey. At the time it was hoped that the factory would open markets in America, and create 150 jobs. After the sod had been turned the site was formally blessed by Fr Michael Barron of St John's, later the PP of the area.

The site of the new factory was on rising ground between a new corporation housing estate and the Waterford Football Ground.

The mastermind behind the new factory was Karel Bacik (grandfather of Senator Ivana Bacik). Previously he had owned and run several glass factories in Czecho-Slovakia producing the famous Bohemian glassware. He survived the Hitler regime uneasily, being forced to produce military glassware. However, after the war it seemed that the steadily encroaching communism of Czecho-Slovakia was not likely to look kindly on his bourgeois status and entrepreneurial skills.

Looking round he remembered an old customer in Dublin, Bernard Fitzpatrick of Nassau Street. Fitzpatrick encouraged him to come to Ireland with the idea of reviving the long-dead Waterford glass tradition. Fitzpatrick had seen the old Waterford crystal in public buildings in Philadelphia, and was convinced that there would be a big market in America for such fine glass.

A few days after the sod-turning, a new company Waterford Glass Ltd was registered in Dublin with a nominal capital of £15,000. Bacik had evidently not left his native country empty-handed.

A few months later his first employee, chief designer Miroslav Havel, arrived, and a few further months later the company began to make glass, initially simply decorating blanks imported from Belgium. In the early days the customers were mainly pubs and hospitals. In November the firm applied to the council for permission to extend the factory—this was the occasion of a blazing row in the council as to whether Czecho-Slovakia was or was not anti-Catholic.

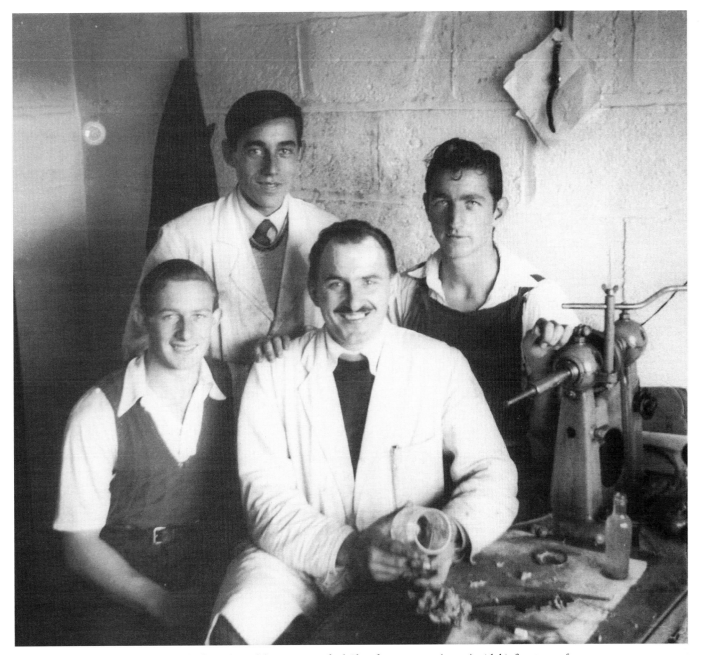

Miroslav Havel the Chief Designer of the new Waterford Glass factory c.1949 (centre) with his first team of engravers
(l–r) Tommy Caulfield, Danny Byrne and Tommy Wall (Courtesy Brian Havel)

The first phase of the revived Waterford Glass was not to last long. Just three years after the sod-turning ceremony, in March 1950 the *Munster Express* reported that Waterford Glass had been taken over by a new group already interested in an allied industry, Irish Glass Bottle. Rumour had it that the Glass Bottle people had been pursuing the young firm for some time, even trying to weaken them by flooding the market with imported glasses. On the other hand, it was undoubtedly true that Waterford Glass was badly in need of new capital.

Leading this new team was the extraordinary figure of Joe McGrath, ex Minister for Labour on the Shannon Scheme, founder and MD of the Hospitals Sweepstake, controller of numerous other businesses, not to mention his stud farms and racehorses.

A new MD, Noel Griffin, was put into the factory which was soon moved to Johnstown. Karel Bacik was given a grand office but no responsibility, and became a rather sad figure in the background.

Waterford Glass, under its new owners, went from strength to strength.

Ballybricken Fair in 1948, where a fair had been held for more than 700 years. A few years later, in 1956, the fair was replaced by a cattle mart.

'At the service of the Waterford smart set'—a window of Shaw's in 1956 (Courtesy Annie Brophy Collection)

General Richard Mulcahy (left) the leader of Fine Gael on a visit home to Waterford in 1948. Shown with Mayor Thaddeus Lynch and City Manager Liam Raftis (Annie Brophy collection).

The Power Brothers of 94 Dominic Place with hurling medals and trophy ca 1950 (Annie Brophy collection)

A May procession in the 1950s (Annie Brophy collection)

Waterford League Winners, 1937 (Annie Brophy collection)

Introducing showbands

On 14 February 1958 'Waterford's up and coming orchestra' The Royal Showband, was advertised as appearing in the Olympia Ballroom on Sunday, from 8 pm to midnight. The name appears in good bold type just under the great band of the day, the Clipper Carlton, from the North, whom many credit with starting the showband craze. The Royal had a bit to go, however: the Clipper Carlton were on on Friday, from 9 pm to 3 am and entrance was 6 shillings. To get into the Olympia for The Royal on Sunday would only cost one shilling and sixpence, and there would be no bar for drinks. This was the last chance for a while to see The Royal, for there was no dancing during Lent, which started on the following Wednesday.

Originally designed and built as a skating rink, the Olympia is best remembered as the mecca of dancing in the south east. (During Lent they re-opened as a skating rink.) The timber floor, so meticulously laid for roller skating, proved ideal for dancing upon and was one of the finest in the country.

A memory of 'The Rink' shared by many people is the 'Parish Social'. In the era before Debs' Balls this was the time when teenagers graduated to the dancing scene. Whether it was the Ballybricken Social or the St John's Social, tickets were always hard to come by. The social life of the city centred on the Olympia and many romances blossomed from there with the question 'Would you like a Jaf-Ora?'

Like halls all over the country, the Olympia lost out with the advance of discos in the 1980s.

The Royal story began in the mid-50s when a group of Waterford youngsters stood in front of the stages at the Olympia and Arundel Ballrooms, with stars in their eyes. They formed a band to have some fun and went on to change the face of Irish music. The name, incidentally, has more to do with the Theatre Royal than Queen Elizabeth!

The Royal Showband in Los Angeles—the Royal were to Waterford what the Beatles were to Liverpool. The showband phenomenon of the late 1950s and 1960s was started in the late 1950s by the Northern Irish band the Clippers. Many of the best-loved names came from Waterford.

They went full time professional in 1959, with Brendan Bowyer giving up his clerk's job in National Paper, to his parents' dismay. By October they were playing five or six nights a week to packed audiences. Bigger ballrooms were being built across the country and they began to play to crowds of 2,000 or more a night.

The Royal was very much a Waterford band, playing to the young workers in the new factories across the city, who lived in the new housing estates. Everyone knew where the band lived, knew their families, saw them around the city.

As the 1950s gave way to the swinging 1960s, The Royal were playing five nights a week and singer Brendan Bowyer was sending young girls wild with his high powered stage show. In many halls crowds fifteen to twenty deep would cram around the stage all night watching the band—many locals will remember the night at the Olympia Ballroom when Brendan went through the floor of the stage during one of his gyrating leaps.

The Royal filled ballrooms all over the country, set new attendance records practically every week, topped the Irish charts more than half a dozen times, became the only Irish band to win the coveted Carl Alan Award in England and later became a huge success in Las Vegas.

Other Waterford bands who were successful both in Ireland and Britain were The Savoy, The Foot-tappers, The Derek Joys, The Decca, The Fleetwoods, The Atlantic, The Seven Seas, The Capri, Frankie King, The Rhythm Kings, Blue Aces, The Valentines, The Woodchoppers, The Roulettes and The Cowboys. Some of the men who guided the bands were Seán and Billy Mulcahy, Hugh Dunphy, George Murphy, Bill Grant and Noel Sinnott.

A view of Ferrybank in 1956

Official portrait of Dick Jones, Mayor of Waterford 1959
(Annie Brophy collection)

The closure of the Tramore railway

It had been rumoured for years that the Tramore railway was likely to close, long before the axe actually fell in September 1960.

The *Munster Express* was of course against the closure, not least because its Editor, J. J. Walsh, was a regular user of the line. 'IS TRAMORE RAILWAY DUE FOR CLOSURE?' ran a front page headline on 2 September, reporting the mounting rumours that the railway was soon to be replaced by a bus service.

A month later, when the expected blow had fallen, the paper reported the declaration by the Mayor of Waterford

that the decision 'must be resisted all the way', and a determination by the Chamber of Commerce to meet with the Chairman of CIE, Todd Andrews.

In October the *Munster Express* declared that it was madness to close the railway with a general election so imminent; that the Tramore line was only losing £3,000 a year, nothing like the loses of the West Clare and West Cork lines; that the road system was nothing like good enough to take all the buses that would be required. If only, the paper declared, CIE really understood the local circumstances.

But to no avail; the secretary of CIE (Seán Lemass's brother Frank) said that no reconsideration was possible. The line was finally closed in December, with the last scheduled service cancelled, to avoid demonstrations.

The Waterford and Tramore railway had by then been trundling up and down the 7¼ mile track for 106 years. With characteristic Victorian speed, the first sod had been cut only in February 1853, with the whole line laid in less than eight months. The inaugural journey took 25 minutes, with the 200 guests clamouring for a rerun before adjourning for a banquet.

The next hundred years of service were to be remarkably safe, with only three serious accidents and one fatality. In 1858 the 6.20 from Tramore failed to stop at the terminus, and crashed through a wall, killing a little girl in the street. It was more than seventy years before the next accident, when the 12.15 from Waterford was derailed at Carriglong Bridge. The injured were quickly attended to by a local doctor and removed to the City and County Infirmary. The cause of this accident was never discovered, though conspiracy theorists have suggested that disaffected Blue Shirts were involved. The next and last accident was in August 1947 when a train failed to stop at Tramore and smashed through the solid brick wall on to Strand Road, Tramore, to the astonishment of holidaymakers.

The Tramore train at Ballindud on the last day of steam on the line, in 1954 (Courtesy Jack O'Neill Collection)

Despite the showers of bricks and masonry no one was hurt.

The sad truth was that, apart from those travelling to work in Waterford from Tramore (including of course the Editor of the *Munster Express*), the demand for the line was limited to the short holiday period. For nine months of the year the line made losses. As early as 1955 changes to rolling stock and engines gave a broad hint that CIE did not intend the line to last. The booking offices were closed except during the summer season, tickets being issued by the guards.

Finally, the Waterford–Tramore line was closed in 1960, in common with Dublin's Harcourt Street Line (closed 1958), the Donegal Railways (1959) and the West Clare (1962). CIE were in fact somewhat ahead of the British Beeching Report (1963) which initiated the close down of a quarter of Britain's rail system.

PART THREE
1961–2010

The 1960s

Flavours of the 1960s
selected by MYRIAM WALSH

Dances and social life
In the 1960s hunt balls and dances were important events in the social calendar. The *Munster Express* reported on hunt balls, beagle balls and military balls, with photographs, and carried advertising for these events. In January 1961 the paper stated that 'the Waterford Hunt Ball was a scintillating success and has lost none of its glitter, glamour and gaiety which has characterised it down the years.' There was a list of the 250 couples present at the ball and the notables included members from the Galway, Limerick, Kilkenny and Tipperary Hunts. Music was by well-known Mick Delahunty and his band. Catering was by Lawlors of Naas who provided for the glitterati at many social and racing occasions in Ireland.

"The Munster Express" WATERFORD. FRIDAY, 12th APRIL, 1963. has a **GREATER CIRCULATION** (net sales) than the **TOTAL** of **ALL** Waterford Papers

QUESTIONS
1—"Blessed is he who has found his work; let him ask no other blessedness." This was written by Carlyle in "Past and Present." Give his first name?
2—How did the Phoenix Park, Dublin, get its name?
3—When was the Irish national system of education established?
4—When does a neap (slack) tide occur?
(Answers at foot of this page?)

The Munster Express

Sgeala Muman

Sixteen Pages

TELEPHONES: 4953 & 4954

Everyone's eating **TAYTO** crisps

Registered at the General Post Office as a newspaper,   EST. 1859. 104th YEAR.   **FRIDAY, 12th APRIL, 1963**   FIRST EDITION ::   PRICE FIVEPENCE

ATLANTIC BALLROOM
TRAMORE
Grand Opening of Season Easter Sunday
— *THE SENSATION OF 1962* —

THE CADETS

Dancing: 9—2. ::   Admission: 6/-
TRANSPORT:
Special All-In Bus Service from Railway Square from 7.30 onwards.
ADMISSION: 7/6 ALL-IN (BUS AND DANCE).

GOODS TRAIN DERAILED

Picture taken at Milltown, Kilmacow, on Wednesday morning, shows part of the derailed goods train, as members of the breakdown gangs from Inchicore Works, Dublin, were busily engaged in clearing the line. Twenty-three wagons were derailed.

HAVEN HOTEL, DUNMORE EAST
Ideal for your Wedding Reception. Our terms include, exclusive use of Hotel Ballroom, All Floral Decorations, Changing Room, Perfect setting for your photographs.

Post of Staff Architect
Waterford Corporation Postpones City Manager's Proposal
"This is being 'Cohooed' In Customs House"— Collr. Power.
"This is being 'coooohed' above in the Customs House in Dublin

Serious Goods Train Derailment
Big Pile-Up At Milltown   gate to let a motorist through, porter she was in bed when,

A pint on St Patrick's Day
In the column 'City Chatter' by Man about Town, we are told that St Patrick's Day 1961 'will go down in history as the day on which you can go down to the local for a pint for the first time in 35 years'. Before the change in the pub licensing laws in 1961, the Dog Show at the RDS was the only place in Ireland where alcohol could be bought on our National Holiday.

Mass cards
Lists of the Mass cards sent to the family on the death of a family member were published in the *Munster Express* during these years.

Bishop's warning
In his Lenten Pastoral of February 1961 the Bishop of Waterford and Lismore Rev. Dr D. Coholan issued a warning against drinking, gambling and vicious habits. He appealed to the young people, suggesting that they put on shorter dances to avoid these practices.

The Clancy Brothers with Tommy Makem

Dirty books
'Really frightening literature fell into the hands of Waterford children' was the headline in the *Munster Express* highlighting a report from a Waterford Corporation meeting. Councillors were informed that some most undesirable literature was coming into Waterford in waste paper cargos.

Local children were raiding the cargos and removing the literature. It was said that CIE were slipping up by not having a watch on the incoming lorries at the wharf. The cargos were thereafter discharged at the Paper Mills jetty in Granagh.

The case of the missing litter bin
A rugby team from Keen in Wales touring Ireland at Easter were accused of stealing one of the new litter bins in Carrick-on-Suir. The chairman of the UDC meeting said he didn't want the matter to reach the press as it was only a rumour. Councillor P. P. Bourke stated 'we must show that we can't allow strangers to come here and do what they like.'

Countering, Councillor R. L. Bourke said, 'There is another litter bin missing now and there is not one Welsh team in town.' Apologies were issued to the Keen Sporting Association on behalf of the Carrick-on-Suir UDC.

The Kilkenny Beer Festival
Over 20,000 people from Ireland, the UK, the US and Europe flocked to the opening of Ireland's first Beer Festival in Kilkenny on 15 May 1964, sponsored by Smithwick's brewery. The brewery is situated on the site of a Franciscan abbey where monks had brewed ale since the 14th century. Smithwick's Brewery, founded by John Smithwick in 1710, is Ireland's oldest operating brewery. Ale continued to be brewed in Kilkenny by the Smithwick family until 1965 when Guinness acquired Smithwick's brewery from Walter Smithwick.

Inspiration for the Kilkenny Beer Festival came in part from the Munich October Fest. A band from Munich was invited over to provide a special German atmosphere. The nominal entrance charge into the Kilkenny Beer Festival gave access to the free beer tent. Two beer tankards were given out to everyone in the beer tent to be able to drink the free Smithwicks ale. The Kilkenny Beer Festival was such a success that over 40,000 appeared on closing day of the week-long event. The festival committee decided to organize another Kilkenny Beer Festival for the following year because of its success. Smithwick's Brewery had got great publicity and it had put the Marble City of Kilkenny on the international map. This festival launched the trend of summer festivals held throughout Ireland to promote tourism and bring revenue to the cities and towns.

The Kilkenny Beer Festival has developed into the Kilkenny Arts Festival, a cultural event of international standing, attracting artists, musicians, historians and writers.

County and City Informary prizegiving 1965—the prizewinnning nurses surrounded by the local great and good

Waterford Festival of Light Opera 'City of colour, glamour and music'

By September 1964 the Festival of Light Opera in Waterford had grown from 11 to 20 nights. 'The 1964 Sixth Festival was opened by Dublin business magnate Senator E. A. McGuire' reported the *Munster Express*.

Senator McGuire made history in Waterford when he offered a priceless complete suite of old 18th-century Waterford glass to the City Corporation at a reception. His father, John F. McGuire, had long associations with Waterford business life. Among the officers of the festival committee present at the reception were President Very Rev. T. Ahearne, PP, Chairman William Carroll and Hon. Treasurer R. O. Milne.

An editorial in the *Munster Express* reported on the light opera festival with the title 'Waterford's place in the sun'.

A controversy concerning the festival arose when the list of festivals in the UK omitted the Waterford Light Opera Festival. The editorial stated that 'Waterford people are quiet and decorous. That, unfortunately, is their outstanding fault. Unlike neighbouring counties they lack aggressiveness'. The Waterford deputy Teddy Lynch criticised Aidan O'Hanlon of Bord Fáilte for the omission, declaring that it would put valuable tourism revenue for Waterford at risk. Deputy Lynch went on to raise the matter in the Dáil.

The Silver Jubilee of Waterford's Municipal Art Gallery

The Jubilee was marked by an art exhibition on 18 September 1964. A hundred works on show were representative of present-day artists with John Keating and George Campbell among them. Paintings by local artists were included in the exhibition. There was a large attendance at this most successful social occasion.

Friends fall out for talking during Mass

In the 1960s Mass-going was a serious matter. A Co. Kilkenny man scolded for talking during Mass assaulted the man who checked him on the steps of the church after Mass. Mr M. M. Halley, solicitor, Waterford, defending his client said that his client 'was very naughty' when he had lost his temper on the morning in question and beat up his friend. The two men made up and the case was dismissed.

Postman panicked

A temporary postman who had hidden 900 letters had been unable to cope with his job and had panicked, a Waterford court was told. The offender was given a six months suspended sentence. It was stated that he had a poor level of literacy and should not have been employed in this capacity in the first place.

New ferry service initiated

The new car ferry service between Rosslare and Fishguard was inaugurated by Mr Erskine Childers, Minister for Transport, at a ceremony in Rosslare. The new service opened up Waterford and surrounding counties to visitors from the UK and was expected to bring considerable revenue from tourism to the region.

The 'Tramore Gossip' column noted that following the opening of the new car ferry service, the number of caravanners increased considerably at the site in Riverstown.

Big crowd at Tramore race

The resort was favoured by fair weather for the Whit weekend race meeting. There was a good attendance and punters were on top on opening day. .

The *Munster Express* column 'Passage and Dunmore Jottings' reported that local jockey Tony Redmond had two winners. A very big crowd had travelled by the local bus service to the two-day meeting.

Tommy Durney (front) and Michael Butch Power on Linotypes

Compositor Tony Rogers checks pages of type in the composing room

Walking race

The walking race from Waterford to Tramore attracted a splendid entry. The course was a test of physical fitness. There were 20 prizes and certificates of physical ability for all participants. All entries were addressed to Mr Fintan O'Byrne, Newtown Hill, Tramore. The entry fee was 2s 6d. The walking race took place on 25 June and first home was S. O'Keefe, Clonmel.

Mrs Bowyer

Elizabeth O'Connor wrote the theatre column for many years. In the edition of 2 July she interviewed Brenda Bowyer, mother of Stanley Bowyer, and grandmother of Brendan Bowyer, lead singer of The Royal Showband. Mrs O'Connor was so impressed by Mrs Bowyer that she entitled the piece 'I met a gracious lady'.

Áine O'Connor

Elizabeth O'Connor was mother of the beautiful, and talented Áine O'Connor who was an RTÉ presenter for some years. As a schoolgirl Áine attended the Ursuline Convent and there won an award for acting. She was the partner of actor Gabriel Byrne, but died tragically young of cancer.

Waterford Hunt Ball goes to Dublin for the first time

A letter from Mr Dayrell Gallway, the Hon. Secretary of the Waterford Hunt Ball Committee, on 18 June, informed the Editor that the Shelbourne Hotel in Dublin had been booked on 5 August for 'the gay and glamorous' Waterford Hunt Ball. The change of venue was to coincide with the Dublin Horse Show week at the RDS. The effort by the earnest and enterprising Waterford committee was aimed at establishing this popular event on the Dublin social calendar.

Important art exhibition in Waterford
The Jack B. Yeats exhibition was opened in Waterford Municipal Art Gallery by Dublin architect Michael Scott FRIAI. Seventeen paintings worth over £62,000 were exhibited. Director of the Arts Council Rev. Donal O' Sullivan had travelled to Waterford for the exhibition and praised the city in his speech saying that 'Waterford Arts Committee has set a noble example and had done remarkable things for the city'. He added that Waterford Arts Committee always received funding because they only asked for it having done their best to raise it by themselves.

Education in Waterford
At a dinner in Dublin an important announcement was made concerning the future of Waterford's oldest Protestant schools, Newtown and Bishop Foy. Mr James Sexton of Tramore, President of the Newtown and Mountmellick Old Scholars Association, stated at the dinner that the schools might amalgamate. A committee was formed to plan a much closer working relationship between the two schools.

The amalgamation took place with the location of the schools in Newtown using the name of Newtown School. Waterford was now at the forefront of Protestant education in Ireland. Newtown School had been founded in 1798 by the Religious Society of Friends (Quakers). The school provides education for boarding and day students of all religious persuasions. The students and staff play an active part in the cultural and sporting life in Waterford.

Student accommodation sought in Tramore for French students
Tramore is a seaside resort favoured by foreign students wishing to learn English during the summer holidays. In 1966 twenty houses were required for July and August to host one student per family. The students were accompanied by a chaperone from Tour Club de France.

The French lady representative from France checking out the suitability of Tramore said she was greatly impressed by what she saw in the seaside resort regarding accommodation and facilities. Tom Reddy of Tramore Town Commissioners said they would fully co-operate in this endeavour. It would be good publicity for the resort and would be seen as a civic and social experience rather than a money profile operation.

Dirty cars
In the 'Letters to the Editor' column, William Phelan suggested a Tidy Street Competition or Tidy Housing Estates Competition. He said that Waterford would become 'such a gay, bright place' by implementing such ideas. Shoppers and shopkeepers should be encouraged to keep their cars clean and students could be employed during the holidays to plant flowers in green spaces.

Lecture
The Old Waterford Society lecture for April 1966 on the Malcolmson family was given by Charles St Jacob at the Tower Hotel and attracted a wide audience of young and old.

Bee keeping promoted
The 'Kilkenny City Topics' column reported that a lecture was given by John Daly, specialist in horticulture and bee keeping from Co. Wexford to the Kilkenny Bee Keeping Society in the Metropolitan Hotel in Kilkenny. It was hoped to create an interest in bee keeping among young people in vocational schools.

Waterpark Rugby Football Club deserved winners in 1966
Waterpark 2nd XV won the Provincial Towns' Cup in
Carlow. The cup was presented to Captain Gerry O' Neill
by Dermot Shalloe, President of the Leinster Branch. In his
speech he said that the Waterford team had been undefeated
in the fourteen games played in the tournament. It was a
great team effort and showed a great team spirit.

Team: F. Kelly, M. Healy, D. Healy, J. Mc Donald, L.
O' Shea, M. Winkle, L. Flynn, T. Meehan, S. Thread,

G. O'Neill, (Captain), P. Flynn, P. Murphy, B. Healy, E.
Kearne.

These rugby players on the Waterpark rugby team were
most popular members on the social scene in the 1960s.
Waterpark Rugby Club held Saturday night dances in the
Haven Hotel, Dunmore East and in the Grand Hotel in
Tramore. Dancing was from 9–12.30 and admission was 5s.
These dances are looked on with nostalgia by those now in
their sixties.

AND NOW — THE SOUTH!

December 23rd is the day for which you have been waiting. For on the evening of that historic day the giant transmitting masts on lonely Mullaghanish and Mount Leinster will beam Telefis Eireann programmes into thousands of homes in Cork and Kerry, Waterford and Wexford, Carlow, Limerick and Tipperary. An historic day, indeed! And what wonderful entertainment there is in store for you. Night after night Telefis Eireann will bring you the cream of Irish talent in music and song, drama and variety, news and sport. There will be many items of local interest such as "A TRUSTY HAVEN"—a 30-minute docu-

mentary on Cork City, special local editions of "THE SCHOOL AROUND THE CORNER" and other items in "BROADSHEET" and in Women's Programmes. In addition you can see many popular international programmes — thrillers, westerns, documentaries, drama. Telefis Eireann has something for everyone.

Ensure that you won't miss the thrill and excitement of opening night: see your television dealer now and have your set installed or adapted in time for December 23rd.

Full Programme details in RTV Guide. Every Friday from your newsagent. Price 6d.

Telefis Eireann

COMING TO YOUR AREA DECEMBER 23

The white portion on the maps shows the area of top-quality reception: good reception will be available over a much wider area.

SPORT   DRAMA   LIGHT ENTERTAINMENT

Friday 21 December, 1962

Tennis tournaments

The senior team of Tramore Tennis Club, represented by senior club members Jeff Cheasty and Noel Purcell from Portlaw and junior tennis member Myriam Walsh from Tramore, won the Tuthill Tennis Cup in Carrick-on-Suir in 1963.

Sunday Tennis Day Cup tournaments held in Waterford city and county, Kilkenny and Tipperary in the 1960s were a great way of getting to know fellow tennis players in the region. Senior and Junior tennis weeks were great sporting and social events in St Anne's Tennis Club in Waterford and Tramore Tennis Club. They attracted tennis players on the circuit from various regions of Ireland.

Water safety

Water Safety Week in Tramore, organised by Miss Dunlop and members of the Red Cross at The Cove in Tramore, provided the opportunity for swimmers to gain badges for water safety in the coastal region and to meet others interested in water sports.

Hunt Ball

The popular Kilmoganny Harriers Hunt Ball took place in the Ormonde Hotel, Carrick on Suir on Wednesday, 19 January. The admission of 30s included a sit down turkey supper and fully licensed bar.

Mick Delahunty and his orchestra provided the music, and dancing was from 9 pm to 4 am. Dress was formal; it was an elaborate social occasion.

Advertisement (1967)

Lough Derg 4 day pilgrimage tour by luxury coach, with the approval of Reverend Monsignor Flood of Lough Derg. All in fare £7 10s from Lismore, Dungarvan, Tramore, Waterford, Carrick-on-Suir, Clonmel includes reserved seat on coach, lunch, dinner, boat and hospice charges. Tickets available from Phelan's travel agency, Clonmel.

The Lough Derg island pilgrimage in Co Donegal is the most arduous of pilgrimages in Ireland. Yet more and more people are doing it.

Vintage and veteran cars visit Waterford

The Mayor of Waterford, Alderman Paddy Browne, welcomed Mrs M. Bianconi, a descendant of Charles Bianconi, during the visit of the Irish Vintage and Veteran Car Club Rally to Waterford.

The 1967 Kilkenny Beer Festival

T. P. Healy of Waterford Crystal sponsored the beer tent at the Kilkenny Beer Festival and presented a cheque and four suites of Waterford glass to Alderman M. J. McGuinness, Mayor of Kilkenny, as prizes for the international greyhound meeting at the Kilkenny Beer Festival. Mr Bill Finnegan was the Chairman of the Festival Committee.

Six hundred ballad groups took part in the international ballad group competition. Parachute jumping and daredevil motor cycle stunts featured among the attractions. Over 300,000 people visited the festival.

However, the name of the festival was criticised by many people. They pointed out that alcohol was not the main feature. Certain fixtures involved no beer.

The Silver Slipper Ballroom

The *Munster Express* of 21 July 1967 noted that the Silver Slipper Ballroom in Tramore put on variety shows twice a week. Good clean fun, catchy singsongs and uncomplicated humour for children and parents enticed holiday makers and locals alike. In the past the Silver Slipper Ballroom had been a skating rink enjoyed by locals in the winter season.

'Best ever at Tramore Golf Club'

This was the headline in the *Munster Express* of 28 July 1967 over a story about the scratch cup and round robin tournament. Tom Cassidy was the only local in the final of the tournament. He was beaten by a golfer from New Ross. The Captain, J. O'Driscoll, and Hon. Sec., J. O. Cantwell said the tournament was the best ever.

In 1966, the standard scratch of Irish courses was revised and among them was Tramore. Up to then, the standard scratch of the seaside course was 74. Now it is 71 and the bogey is 72.

Sindy, the baby elephant

The circus was an important feature in the social and entertainment calendar of the area. Sindy, the two-year-old baby elephant, was the star attraction at Fossetts Circus in Poleberry in Waterford, much to the delight of the young attendance . There were four performances in Waterford before the circus went out to Tramore for an extended run

Fossetts Circus is the oldest circus in Ireland and is family owned. Nowadays it does not travel with live animals.

The 1960s era in the *Munster Express*

The 1960s was one of the best decades in the history of Waterford. As the economy expanded, Waterford was well positioned, so employment grew and emigration slowed down as industries expanded. The showband era had started and there was a general feel-good factor.

The *Munster Express* prospered in this period, too, with the newspaper pages rising to 16 and 18 pages per week with lots of news and national advertising from Nescafé and Beechams to beer and cigarettes. Mick Delahunty and The Royal showbands were advertised. In Christmas 1962

the advertising scene changed completely, with the launch of RTÉ in a blaze of publicity. Previously, national brands wanting to access Waterford audiences had to use the local paper, now they could get a big audience all across the country by TV. As a result, many national ads migrated to TV. For the *Munster Express*, this was really as new as the internet is today.

Court cases figured much on the front page; assault was the main crime, often due to too much drink. There is a different news diet today, drugs and hold-ups are more common, in those days they were only in the movies.

Waterford had many cinemas—the Regal, Savoy, Coliseum, the Ritz, New Ross and the Rex, Tramore, as well as the Strand in Carrick; there was much to choose from for entertainment with even a dancers' column in the newspaper.

Golf socials were big with one heading in spring that year saying 'Golf Club members go gay' as they enjoyed themselves at a function.

Land sales became big news as the property market grew with St Patrick's Park Newtown being sold. This was the site of the first airplane flight in Waterford back in 1913 with Corbett Wilson and was also the site of the Waterford Show; the King of England had visited that show eight years earlier.

The biggest single event of the decade was the 1963 visit of President Kennedy to Ireland. John F. Kennedy came to Ireland to visit his ancestors in Dunganstown, Co. Wexford, near New Ross. J. J. Walsh, Editor, had a connection with the US Democrat party through Jim O'Brien of Tramore and because of that had the opportunity to meet the President on a few occasions, going to Dublin for his arrival and to New Ross—the *Munster Express* covered these events extensively.

The visit was described as 'the home-coming' as New Ross rose to the occasion in grand manner, with scenes of tremendous enthusiasm, with the carnival town extending an unprecedented welcome. Referring to the Cuban missile crisis of the previous year, Andrew Minihan, Chairman of New Ross UDC, described Kennedy as 'the President of Peace'. Photographs in the paper showed Labour Mayor Tom Brennan, with Eugene Shriver and Jean Kennedy Smith, later US Ambassador to Ireland, who would pay a courtesy visit to the *Munster Express* and Waterford during her term.

Later that year, the world was shaken by Kennedy's assassination. Prionsias Mac Aonghusa wrote a eulogy and an editorial describing this as a cruel blow to the USA, Ireland and the world.

The 1960s were a time of great expansion of Waterford Crystal, tourism and general industry as the relaxation of trade tariffs boosted Irish economic growth. Of course organised labour looked for a fair share of the benefits, and Waterford had many industrial difficulties. Paper mills, flour mills and meat factories all had disputes.

In 1966 Waterford FC won the FAI League Championship for the first time, winning 11 matches in a row to snatch the title. They won it again in 1968 and almost made the double with 40,000 watching the final against old rivals Shamrock Rovers.

Later that year there was a magnificent tie against European Cup winners Manchester United. The home leg of the first round tie was played in Lansdowne Road, Dublin before 60,000 spectators. Waterford lost 3–1 with Denis Law doing the business for United and Johnny Matthews replying for Waterford. The return leg in Old Trafford was lost 7–1.

The county hurlers started the decade fresh from All Ireland victory in 1959 and reached the final again in 1963. Croke Park was packed with 65,000 spectators but the team lost to arch rivals Kilkenny by a margin of 3 points. This was the highest scoring final ever and a great thrill for all the spectators who made the game. Remarkably, neither the score nor news of the game was on the front page of the *Munster Express*. They were relegated to sports page 12.

The violence in Northern Ireland marred the end of the decade. Although Waterford was not close to the border, bomb scares and an influx of people from the six counties here did affect the city.

SOCCER JUNIOR

RESULTS:

Infirmary Cup (Final)—Bolton 4. Castle 0.

Minor League—Kilmacthomas 0, Crusaders 4.

Factory League—E.M.C. 2, Munster Chipboard 1; Waterford Glass A 2, Portlaw Tanners 0; Builders 0, Cherrys 1; Waterford Foundry 3, Flour Mills 2; Paper Mills B 6, E.S.B. 3; Builders 2, Tyresoles 2; H. Denny A 1, H. Denny B 1; Flahavan Mills 1, A.C.E.C. 0.

FIXTURES:

Friday, 28th June:
Ozier Park, 8 o'c., Factory League—Paper Mills A v. Goldcrust.
Marian Park, 8 o'c., Division II—Bohemians v. Southend.

Sunday, June 30:
Ozier Park, 8 o'c.—E.M.D. v. Paper Mills A.

Monday, July 1st:
Ozier Park, 8 o'c.—H. Dennys v. Foundry.

Tuesday, July 2nd:
Ozier Park, 8 o'c.—Accountants v. Builders.

BOLTON INFIRMARY CUP

Bolton crowned a great Infirmary Cup campaign with a convincing nil win in their final tie with Castle. They were undoubtedly flattered by the score for Castle had as great a share of the exchanges and played some delightful football but found as did other clubs in this competition, that Bolton's defence was almost impregnable. Ted O'Regan was again brilliant in goal and his save from a Collins shot midway in the second half when the score was one nil, was the turning point of the game.

WORLD NEWS

Mr. Krushchev and his wife left Moscow this morning and are expected to arrive in East Berlin to-morrow. The Russian Leader is paying an official visit in honour of Herr Ulbricht, the East German Foreign Minister who celebrates his 70th birthday this week.

At the end of the first 18 holes of the Irish Amateur Golf Championship, Joe Carr (Sutton) and Eric O'Brien (U.C.D.) were all square. Carr squared at the 11th and from then on it was touch and go. O'Brien captured the 17th but Carr produced another 2 at the short 18th to level again.

The first witness called by the prosecution in the case against Dr. Stephen Ward, the London osteopath, was Christine Keeler. Mr. Mervyn Griffith-Jones, Counsel for the prosecution, said he would have to mention names of perfectly respectable people as well as others in this case. He asked that the names of respectable persons should not be disclosed.

The death occurred suddenly of Senator Daniel J. Moloney of Listowel, Co. Kerry. Deceased, was a member of the Fianna Fail Party, was also a member of Kerry Co. Council and Chairman of its Housing Section, as well as other public bodies.

Christy O'Connor and Kel Nagle led in the opening round of the Dunlop Masters Golf Tournament at Aston, Birmingham, this morning. O'Connor reached the turn in 34, 1 stroke behind Nagle. The Irishman finished with 69.

At the end of the first part of the 6th stage of the Tour de France, Shay Elliott of Ireland, retained the yellow jersey of the overall leader.

————0-0————

Friday 28 June, 1963

In 1963 President Kennedy, the hero of the Cuba crisis, the symbol of youth and widening possibilities to all young Irishmen and women, arrived in Dublin airport. During his three-day stay, Kennedy visited Dublin, Wexford, Cork, Limerick and Galway. In Wexford the President was shown 'documentary proof of the rebel blood of his ancestors.' These were the prison records of a distant cousin who once spent two months in hard labour in Wexford Jail in 1888 for resisting arrest and obstructing the sheriff. At Galway the Mayor spoke his words of welcome entirely in Irish and Kennedy matched the moment. He 'rounded off his address by telling the crowd that if they ever went to Washington and told the man at the gate that they were from Galway, there would be a Céad Míle Fáilte for them.' In New Ross he had tea with a smiling group of his Kennedy cousins.

THE PRESIDENT'S ADDRESS

President John Fitzgerald Kennedy addressing the large gathering at New Ross Quay yesterday (Thursday).

Homecoming Of President Kennedy

NEW ROSS RISES TO THE OCCASION IN THE GRAND MANNER

SCENES OF TREMENDOUS ENTHUSIASM

Carnival Town Extends Unprecedented Welcome

As had happened in Dublin on Wednesday night, when he was given one of the most rousing receptions ever accorded to a distinguished visitor to this country, U.S. President John Fitzgerald Kennedy received a tremendous welcome when yesterday (Thursday) morning he visited New Ross, the ancient and historical County Wexford town from which his great-grandfather took the emigrant ship over 150 years ago. With lavish displays of flags, flowers, bunting and a wide variety · of artistic and ingenious decorations, the town presented a picture of gay, carnival appearance.

From O'Kennedy Park, where the four helicopters of the U.S. Army carrying the President and his entourage from Dublin, arrived at 11.07, eight minutes before schedule, the route along which the motorcade passed on its way to the platform on the Quay was densely thronged with wildly exultant, flag-waving crowds, who comprised only sections of the thousands who took part in the never-to-be-forgotten and never-previously-equalled celebrations.

Before the Presidential car and motorcade left O'Kennedy Park — named in 1953 after Sean O'Kennedy, the town's most famous athlete, who won an All-Ireland Hurling Championship medal in 1910 and four All-Ireland Football Championship medals from 1915 to 1918—the President was met by a reception party consisting of Mr. Gerry Donovan, Vice-Chairman, New Ross U.D.C.; Right Rev. James Monsignor Browne, D.C.L., P.P., V.G., New Ross; Mr. Patrick J. Dolan, Chairman, New Ross Harbour Commissioners; Councillor Murt Buckley, of the Irish Army, and Mr. Richard V. Fitzpatrick, Town Clerk, New Ross.

FREE WORLD LEADER. Addressing the President, Mr. Donovan said: "Welcome, Mr. President; welcome to New Ross. May I say, on behalf of the people of New Ross and of Co. Wexford that we are honoured ...

Band, joined in the singing of "When you wrote to us on the Irish airs, while 100 boys from day of your Inauguration that the New Ross C.B.S., under Rev. you hoped to be with us in the Br. J. N. Murphy, remained in near future, we thought it was the formation of a tableaux which, seen from the air by the arriving helicopters, portrayed ...

Page Ten · Munster Express · Friday, 28th June, 1963

All-Conquering Tour Of U.S. President

VISITS ANCESTRAL HOME NEAR NEW ROSS

TUMULTUOUS WEST GERMAN AND IRISH RECEPTIONS

Greeted By Exulting, Surging Crowd

UNPRECEDENTED SCENES IN DUBLIN AND COUNTY WEXFORD

TO describe adequately the well-nigh indescribable scenes associated with the ten-day European tour of America's first Catholic President — and, incidentally, the first visit to Ireland of any occupant of his exalted position while actually holding the office —would tax the most polished pen of a gifted descriptive writer.

It all began on Sunday last, when the President of his party of 211 people—they included Secretary of State, an Ambassador, an Admiral, two Generals, and 111 reporters and cameramen..were given what was characterised as a "fantastic welcome" from more than 500,000 West Germans in Cologne and Bonn. En route to the latter city from Wahn Airport, they passed through a carnival atmosphere, and mounted police had to force back the record-breaking crowds as they surged towards the smiling, waving President. The crowd jamming Bonn's cobbled market-place was said to be one of the biggest ever seen there.

ROARED APPROVAL.

And how they roared approval as the President gave them a pledge that U.S. forces would stay in Europe as long as they are needed, and promised them that the U.S. would continue to bear a fair share in the "fight for freedom" in a great half-circle stretching from Berlin to Saigon.

"Our unity," he declared, "was forged in a time of danger. It must be maintained in a time of peace. Our alliance was founded to deter a new war. It must now find a way to a new peace. Our strategy was born in a divided Europe, but it must look to the goal of European unity and an end to the divisions of peoples and countries.'

COLOGNE CATHEDRAL.

The excitement reached a peak in wild scenes outside the world-famous Cologne Cathedral, where the President attended High Mass. In the scramble, the Cathedral doors were locked on some dignitaries, including Mr. McGhee, U.S. Ambassador to West Germany. Guards had hurriedly barred the massive doors to prevent a crush of onlookers pressing into the Cathedral after the President and Dr. Adenauer—and it was some time before the stranded members of the official party were able to get in.

TEN-DEEP CROWDS.

In the Rhineland Capital, firecrackers and a police band heralded his arrival. Later, while he was the guest of honour at a dinner given by the West German Chancellor, crowds stood up to ten deep at the entrance to the Chancellory grounds, waving paper flags, cheering and whistling approval as the President drove in his open car, which was brought over from Washington.

On Monday, the President began talks with Dr. Adenauer. On Wednesday, he flew to Berlin to have a firsthand look at the divided city, before leaving for this country.

ECLIPSED IN DUBLIN.

The scenes of overflowing joy and unrestrained enthusiasm witnessed in Western Germany were completely eclipsed on Wednesday evening when the Boeing jet carrying the Presidential party touched down on Dublin Airport's main runway. For President Kennedy, it was the beginning of a threeday programme so gruelling in its demands that it could be undertaken only by a person of his dynamic energy and remarkably determined calibre. The fact that it will be followed immediately by visits to Britain and Italy will make it still more exacting.

stration of his own people's deeply-rooted affection, by which his whirlwind itinerary is being highlighted. Everywhere he went, the same stirring scenes were repeated; he passed through richly-garlanded, be-flagged and bunting - streamered highways lined by countless thousands, all anxious to get a glimpse of the Presidential party.

In operation, too, were the most widespread security operations ever undertaken to ensure the safety of a visitor, the measures taken in this country in that respect being augmented by the President's own bodyguard, which accompanied him everywhere.

From Santry all the way to O'Connell Bridge, and along the quays to Parkgate tSreet, every conceivable vantage point had been booked by thousands of people who were taking no chances about the weather. In O'Connell Street, hundreds of Gardai were assigned to mak sure that the thronging crowds would not overflow through specially-erected barriers.

21-GUN SALUTE.

Immediately President Kennedy stepped from his aircraft, army trumpeters and drummers heralded his arrival to the waiting throng. The first official welcome came from President E. de Valera. This was followed by that of An Taoiseach (Mr. Lemass) and the American Ambassador, Mr. Matt McCloskey.

President Kennedy then received the greetings of members of the Government, the Diplomatic Corps, the Chief of Staff, Lieut-General Sean McKeown and high-ranking Army officers. The crowds on the tarmac next faced the Tricolour and Stars and Stripes for the respective National Anthems, played by the No. 1 Army Band.

Before the visiting President walked through a troop-lined path to the airport lounge to prepare for the drive through the city, a 21-gun salute, fired at intervals of five seconds, was given.

OFFICIAL PARTY.

President Kennedy's official party includes his sister Mrs. Eunice Shriver; the Secretary of State, Mr. Dean Rusk; the Assistant Secretary of State for European Affairs, Mr. Robert J. Manning; the Director of the State Department's German Desk, Mr. Robert C. Creel; the President's Special Assistant for National Security Affairs, Mr. McGeorge Bundy.

The White House Special Counsel, Mr. Theodore C. Sorensen; the President's Appointment sSecretary, Mr. P. Kenneth O'Donnell; his Military Aide, Major-General Chester V. Clifton; his Air Force Aide, Brig.-General Godfrey T. McHugh; his Naval Aide, Capt. Tazewell T. Shepard (Junr.); Mr. Bundy's Assistant, Mr. David Klein, and

temporary home of a President of the U.S., who is of Irish ancestry, provided a most extraordinary reversal of historic fortune. In the days of the British regime, it was the home of the Chief Secretary—the man whose word was law when this American President's forbears went into exile from an impoverished Ireland. It was the harshness of the edicts which issued from this house that drove the Kennedys and the Fitzgeralds to take the emigrant ship for the great and free Republic of the West.

And here, a few personal details regarding President Kennedy will not be inappropriate. To-day, he is one of America's richest men, with many and magnificent residences. He occupies the White House in Washington, he owns a fabulous home at Cape Cod in Massachusetts, an ancestral home in Boston, a hunting retreat at Camp David, Maryland; two more at Middlesburg, and on Rattle Snake Mount in Virginia. He has the use of his father's splendid mansion at Palm Beach, Florida, and he has a Presidential suite in the Hotel Carlyle in New York City.

SALARY GOES TO CHARITY.

President Kennedy has a yearly salary and expense account of £50,000. He spends £14,000 annually in travelling, and gets £250,000 yearly for the upkeep of the White House. He has a cabin cruiser that costs £28,000 to keep in commission, and more than £200,000 is spent every year in providing him with 'planes and helicopters. He is believed to be the richest President in American history, with a personal fortune of £70 million. Financiers have calculated that he is living at a rate of slightly more than £3 million a year. His annual salary is given wholly to charity—a fact which recently caused him much annoyance when it was disclosed.

When he leaves Ireland, en route for Britain and Italy, he will carry away with him five scrolls, testifying to the fact that he has been made an Honorary Freeman of Dublin, Wexford, New Ross, Galway and Limerick. While these honours confer no perquisites now, they would have been of great value had they been conferred on President Kennedy's ancestors.

NEWSPAPERMEN ARE NEWS.

It is said of newspapermen that they are not news, rather do they make it. The visit of President Kennedy was one occasion when they became news in our Republic. This was so because of the huge number of television personnel and reporters who covered the historic occasion. In all, about 650 Pressmen, TV reporters and cameramen were engaged on the biggest event to happen in Ireland for many years.

A section of the large attendance.

A general view of the scene at New Ross Quay during President Kennedy's visit.

HOMECOMING OF PRESIDENT KENNEDY

(continued from page 1)

which was drawn up alongside the platform. The choir then sang a number of Irish airs, which were enthusiastically received by the crowds.

EXCHANGED GREETINGS.

Before leaving for the ancestral homestead in Dunganstown, Mr. Kennedy walked around the steel barriers which had been erected in front of and at each side of the platform, and, to the ecstacy of the privileged ones, he shook hands and exchanged greetings with a large section of the crowd.

As he left New Ross in his open car, the President was almost mobbed by the excited admirers, who pushed forward in their hundreds to shower their expressions of appreciation on him and give him a rousing send-off at Dunganstown.

THOSE ON THE PLATFORM.

Amongst those on the platform were: Mr. Frank Aiken, Minister for External Affairs, who accompanied the President from Dublin; Rt. Rev. Monsignor Browne; Rt. Rev. Dr. W. P. McAdoo, Protestant Bishop of Ferns, Ossory and Leighlin; Very Rev. Wm. Murphy, P.P., Rosbercon; Very Rev. J. A. Power, O.S.A., Acting Prior, Augustinian Priory, New Ross; Rev. Br. Leo Kennedy, Principal, New Ross C.B.S.; Rev. A. M. Broughton Mills, Rector, St. Mary's, New Ross; Ald. Thomas Brennan (Mayor of Waterford) and Mrs. Brennan;

ure at being back from hence I came. There is an expression in Washington that there are no Kennedys left in Ireland—that they are all in Washington. I wonder are there any Kennedys in this audience? Could they hold up their hands? I am glad to see there are a few who did not catch the boat.

REMEMBER IRELAND!

"It seems to me," said the President, "in these dangerous days, when the struggle for freedom is world-wide against an armed doctrine, that Ireland, in its experience, has one special significance, and that is that the people are able to maintain their national identity and strong faith, and, therefore, those who may feel that in these difficult times freedom may be on the run, or that some nations may be permanently subjugated, would do well to remember Ireland.

"I am proud to come here for another reason, because it makes me even prouder of my own country. My country welcomed many sons and daughters of so many countries and gave them a fair chance and a fair opportunity. A Speaker of the House of Representatives is Irish; the Leader of the Senate is of Irish descent. What is true of the Irish is true of dozens of other peoples. In Ireland, I think you see something of what is so great of the United States. I must say

through gaily garlanded thoroughfares and tightly-packed masses of people, who lined the entire route, waved flags, and shouted themselves hoarse.

The same scenes were repeated when, having had the Honorary Freedom of the City conferred on him, and with all the accompanying ceremonial and addresses, the motorcade was re-formed and proceeded to the Corporation Sports Field, where the Presidential party rejoined their helicopters for the return journey to Dublin.

LUNCH WITH PRESIDENT.

Back in the Capital, President Kennedy lunched with President de Valera and the Taoiseach, Mr. Sean Lemass, at the U.S. Embassy residence. He, later, left the Embassy by car to lay a wreath at Arbour Hill. Thence, through densely-crowded sidewalks, he drove to Leinster House, where history was made when he addressed a joint session of both Houses of the Oireachtas.

HONORARY DEGREES.

This unique ceremony was followed by the conferring of Honorary Degrees at the National University of Ireland and the University of Dublin (Trinity College) and the Honorary Freedom of the City of Dublin at St. Patrick's Hall, Dublin Castle.

At 8 o'clock to-night, President Kennedy will attend a private dinner given by President de Valera at Arus Uachtarain.

To-morrow (Saturday), he will go to Galway, where another great welcome awaits him.

The newly-elected Mayor of Waterford, Alderman Thomas Brennan, was introduced to President Kennedy's two sisters. They are here seen with the Mayor: Mrs. Eunice Shriver (on left) and Mrs. Jean Smith.

The Royal Showband

The rise of the most famous of the showbands, The Royals, on the eve of the 1960s, is directly connected to the changes sweeping the social and economic life of Waterford. The medieval city was energised as never before by an economic revival. Factories sprang up around the city in line with the national transformation from a rural, homogenous society to an urbanised-industrialised society.

Housing estates were built in Waterford to cater for factory workers who, unlike the 1950s generation, did not have to emigrate to make a decent living. People could afford to stay home for the first time. They had more money and were able to socialise on week nights. They wanted to dance to a different tune. Suddenly a bunch of good-looking city kids were jumping around the stage and singing chart hits.

The Royals started as part-timers in 1957, taking their ideas, especially the importance of brass instruments—saxophone, trumpet and trombone—from the Northern band The Clippers. The name, incidentally, owes more to the Theatre Royal than to anyone living in Buckingham Palace. Their first break was in 1957 when they negotiated a gig at the Olympia Parnell Street on St Patrick's night 1958. For another year they played as semi-professionals, working by day and earning £5 each a night when they played. During the day, Brendan Bowyer and Tom Dunphy

The Royal Showband in 1957, at the very start of their career. The picture was taken in the Bowyers' Pub in Baileys New Street, Waterford (l–r) Brendan Bowyer, lead singer and saxophone player, later South Parade; Gerry Cullen, keyboard player, Ferrybank; Charlie Matthews, drummer, Ferrybank; Jim Conlon, banjo and guitar player, Cork Road; Michael Coppinger, saxophone and band leader plus accordion, Ferrybank; Tom Dunphy, St John's Park, bass player and singer

worked as sales clerks in the Paper Mills. In the quiet of his bedroom Brendan Bowyer practised the moves that would drive the girls crazy. Elvis Presley was his great influence.

They went full-time on Easter Sunday 1959. By November, they were playing five or six nights a week, to audiences of 2,000 or more. The crowds swelled further in the early 1960s, and the band's earnings grew accordingly. During Lent, when the ballrooms were closed, The Royals went overseas, to England and to the United States. In late summer 1963 they had their first Irish no 1 hit record, *Kiss Me Quick,* and another at Christmas time, *No More.* In 1964 their hit *Bless Me* stayed in the charts for nearly three months. Their best-known song *The Hucklebuck* was issued in 1965. Astonishingly, this song reappeared in the charts when it was reissued in 1976 and 1981. All the time the band were pushing a gruelling schedule, criss-crossing the country on the not-brilliant roads: Sligo today, then Dublin, then back to Waterford, then perhaps Cork. At a time when the Taoiseach Seán Lemass earned £4,000 a year, it was estimated that the band earned over £100,000 in 1965 in ballroom returns alone. It came as a considerably shock when the Revenue slapped in a demand for £25,000 in back taxes.

Young Brendan Bowyer was a rock n' roller. Couples organised their dates around the movements of The Royal. She wanted to see Brendan, so he took her along. The Royal were a city band. Everyone knew where they lived and recognised them at sight. Band members and even their families were in some way touched by stardom. They were the celebrities of their neighbourhoods, symbols of the new sense of freedom, optimism and prosperity. People who walked past Dunphy's home at St John's Park, or Bowyer's in South Parade, craned their necks in the hope of glimpsing a star. That celebrity status was confirmed when they began to make regular TV appearances. The Royal brought glamour and excitement to Waterford. 'Everybody was delighted that at last we had something that we could take pride in', says Waterford chronicler Eddie Wymberry.

Going from strength to strength in Ireland, The Royals then tried their luck in Los Angeles, flying west just after Christmas and back to Ireland in July. But by the early 1970s the original energy was beginning to wane, and newer bands with new musical styles were appearing all the time. Eventually, Brendan Bowyer and Tom Dunphy decided to re-create themselves, and the old Royal Showband disbanded in July 1971.

Source Vincent Power *Send 'em home sweatin'*

Waterford's golden hurling generation 1957–63 *by* DERMOT KEYES

Between 1957 and 1963, Waterford won an All-Ireland title, were runners-up in the '57 and '63 deciders, and won three Munster titles, a National Hurling League ('63) and the Oireachtas Tournament in 1962.

Despite these successes, did the great Waterford team, the 'golden generation' for hurling in this county, under-achieve? 'I wouldn't think that way at all about that team,' said Frankie Walsh, when interviewed by the *Munster Express* in July 2002.

'You have to remember there were lots of great teams around at the time we were playing. It's often been said to me by different people from around the country that that particular Waterford team should have won three or four All-Irelands. And maybe we should have.

'I always thought that '57 and '63 were the ones we should have won. In '59 I thought we'd played very well in the first match but didn't play as well in the replay and won.

'And when you win an All-Ireland by eight points, I don't think any of us were about to start complaining about how we'd played. We just had the bit of luck we needed that day to win.'

In the *Munster Express* coverage of the '59 heroes' homecoming, our correspondent estimated that a crowd numbering 20,000 turned out to welcome rare hurling bedfellows Waterford and Liam MacCarthy. Bonfires were lit across the city and county, with one blazing brightly atop Mount Misery (above the railway station), a chunk of rock whose ownership is contested by Kilkenny and Waterford GAA fans to this day.

'This victory,' the paper wrote, 'was made all the sweeter by virtue of the hard road travelled to attain it. The hurling might of Galway [then hurling in the Munster Championship], Tipperary, Cork and now Kilkenny have fallen in the wake of this greatest-ever Waterford combination, and in a manner which unmistakably earns them the highest plaudits of the Gaelic world.'

The starting Waterford team in the 1959 All-Ireland Final was as follows: Ned Power, Joe Harney, Austin Flynn, John Barron, Mick Lacey, Martin Óg Morrissey, John Condon, Seamus Power, Philly Grimes, Mick Flannelly, Tom Cheasty, Frankie Walsh (Captain), Larry Guinan, Tom Cunningham, John Kiely.

An All-Ireland winner at centre-forward in Waterford's maiden All-Ireland senior hurling championship victory in 1948, Mount Sion's John Keane coached his county to a second Liam MacCarthy Cup win 11 years later. Widely identified as one of the most stylish and complete inter-county units of the 20th century, that they reached hurling's summit only once understates their greatness.

At the time Keane was described as 'unassuming to the point of self-effacement in public'. His was a team full of names that resonate through the decades of heartache that have subsequently followed at All-Ireland level.

Like the famed Munster team which defeated the All Blacks at Thomond Park in 1978, the names of Waterford's All-Ireland heroes roll off the tongue to this day.

The irrepressible Frankie Walsh of Mount Sion, still hale and hearty, led his team to victory that glorious summer. Among his white-clad comrades stood the teak tough Philly Grimes, and hurling greats such as Martin Óg Morrissey, Larry Guinan, Austin Flynn and Mick Flannelly.

But one man stands out above them all, a true hurling colossus, a hurler as revered in Kilkenny today as he is in his native Waterford. He inspired one of Mícheál O'Hehir's great moments of GAA commentary as he broke through a Kilkenny defence, whose 'defenders [were] falling around him like dying wasps'. That man, the late, great Tom Cheasty, was, in Mícheál Ó Muircheartaigh's phrase, 'an unforgettable Waterford gladiator'.

The Déise faithful awaits a third such triumph.

Waterford FC *v* Manchester United
by MATT KEANE

During the glory period of the 1960s and early 1970s, the Blues made the name of our city and county well known in such diverse places as Istanbul, Budapest, Berlin and Nicosia, but it was the pairing with The Red Devils that still holds a special place in many people's hearts.

The League Championship in 1966 was followed a year later by an extraordinary three in a row, and after another year by two more titles. Only a single point in 1971 stood between Waterford FC and the possibility of an unprecedented six titles on the trot. A magic Blues team made up of magic players.

The first time Waterford qualified for the European Cup they were drawn against Vorwaerts of Berlin (East Germany at the time)—not the best of rewards for winning the League of Ireland for the first time ever. However, in 1968 they drew the mighty Manchester United, the reigning European champions. Ten years earlier many of the Busby Babes perished in the Munich air disaster, and that tragedy had struck a chord with many Irish people. Ten years after the air disaster, Manchester United became the first club from England to win the European Cup, beating Benfica at Wembley with goals from Bobby Charlton (2), George Best and Brian Kidd.

For Waterford followers dreams came true when the first round draw of the European Cup for the season 1968–69 was made. They were paired with this brilliant United team that had lifted the famous trophy four months previously. Nothing like this had ever happened before in Irish football. Not only Waterford people but the entire Irish nation was caught up with the up-coming fixture.

The only problem was that Manchester were drawn first, meaning that they would have home advantage in the first game at Old Trafford. When Waterford played Vorwaerts they played the home leg in Dalymount Park but even that famous Dublin soccer venue would not be capable of holding the crowd who would want to see United play. J. J. Walsh, who was a director of Waterford FC and also a keen follower of rugby, suggested that the match be played in Lansdowne Road which could accommodate 60,000 spectators. So Don Kennedy and the directors, including secretary Dick O'Brien, made an approach to the IRFU and history was made when the first ever soccer game was played at Lansdowne Road, the forerunner of all the International soccer fixtures that have since taken place there, despite opposition from the FAI and Bohemians FC, the landlords of Dalymount.

Ticket prices
When the Waterford club put the tickets for the match on sale they were bombarded with requests from all over

George Best spins the ball round Noel Griffin, European Cup tie, Lansdowne Road 1968

the country, from Cork to Donegal, from Kerry to Sligo. Needless to say, Waterford people wanted their quota. The Waterford directors somehow managed to work a miracle which would have put the loaves and fishes scenario in the shade. Waterford wanted to charge 5s ground admission, but the FAI refused permission, on the grounds that 4s was the price for such a fixture. So 4s it was, much more, of course, for the stands, 10s and 12s for those who opted for covered accommodation. The all-ticket affair packed 45,000 fans into Lansdowne Road on a balmy September evening.

The kick off was at 5.45 pm. Thousands of people left Waterford from early morning determined to enjoy this wonderful occasion. The vast majority, of course, came to see the visitors. Six special trains left Waterford that day, in addition to dozens of buses and hundreds of cars.

Denis the Menace

Waterford lost the game 3–1 but it mattered not. It was the occasion that counted, and the sense of history that accompanied it, as the name of Waterford reverberated through these islands and way beyond. Denis Law, a truly superb player who sadly missed the European Cup Final four months earlier because of injury, scored a hat-trick against Peter Thomas on that never-to-be-forgotten evening. George Best also scored a wonderful goal but it was disallowed because Denis was standing in an offside position.

Vinny Maguire, the Waterford manager, had to decide who would mark George Best. He decided to place Noel Griffin at left full-back with Paul Morrissey making way. The Waterford team was as follows: Peter Thomas, Peter Bryan, Noel Griffin, Vinny Maguire, Jackie Morley, Jimmy McGeough, Al Casey, Alfie Hale, John O'Neill, Shamie Coad and Johnny Matthews. The little Coventry-born winger was the player who scored the Blues goal. Matthews also scored against Celtic in 1971. He also found the net against Real Madrid in 1981 when he was playing for Limerick, only for the goal to be disallowed.

Vinny Maguire left himself out for the second leg in Old Trafford and brought back Paul Morrissey, with Noel Griffin moving to centre-half. Manchester United won that game 7–1 and again it was Denis Law who proved to be Waterford's tormentor as he scored four goals. Francis Burns, Nobby Stiles and Bobby Charlton were the other United goalscorers on Wednesday, 2 October 1968.

The late Al Casey netted the Waterford consolation. During the second leg the Manchester United and Republic of Ireland full-back Tony Dunne clattered into Al Casey. The gifted little Waterford player was lying on the ground in agony. 'Get up, you're OK,' said Dunne. 'It's alright for you to say that', replied Al as Dunne stood over him. 'I'm on the 4 to 12 shift in the Paper Mills tomorrow while you'll be out playing golf.'

Waterford's last League of Ireland title came in season 1972–3. A few First Division titles have been won but a whole generation of Blues followers have never known what it is like to be kings in the land. For those who do know, it remains a lovely dream.

1969: A year of strife

Early 1969 saw 2,000 workers in eight local factories given protective notice because of a dispute involving maintenance fitters and Texaco workers. In February 1969, workers employed by Henry Denny and Sons, Bacon Curers, were laid off because there were not enough animals available at competitive prices. At around the same time, Fismar Ltd began a pilot production run of Badedas, the world-famous bubble bath, at their factory on the Industrial Estate. Also in March 1969, Irish Universal Glass Ltd ceased production at their factory in Lombard Street. They had been manufacturers of crystal cut glass and employed 25 people.

Taoiseach Jack Lynch and his wife Maírín visited Waterford during the 1969 General Election campaign. The Chamber of Commerce came out in active support of moves to erect a second bridge over the River Suir in the city—a campaign that culminated forty years later with the opening of Waterford City Bypass.

It was announced in July 1969 that the first classes in the new Regional Technical College would begin in September of that year with the official opening pencilled in for April 1970.

1972: crowds gather outside the Munster Express *office, some in support, some in protest, as Taoiseach Jack Lynch visits the Editor*

July 1969 brought space into focus with Neil Armstrong becoming the first person on the moon. Here, too, there was a Waterford connection: samples of moon dust were brought back by the US astronauts to be weighed in a remotely controlled electric balance manufactured by Torsion Balance Ltd on the Industrial Estate.

Short-time working was introduced for 400 Jute Factory employees in October 1969 as export orders fell. Waterford Chamber of Commerce decided late in 1969 that women should be allowed to attend their annual dinner in 1970 for the first time in its 182-year history. Women's involvement featured again as Margaret Walsh of Dunmore East made a small piece of social history in November 1969 when she became the first woman in this area to be appointed as a CIE bus driver.

In the same month, Waterford Corporation bought a large tract of land at Kilbarry, Waterford, for the equivalent of £890 per acre. The Corporation was obviously in acquisitive form as it bought the 200-year-old Bishop Foy Palace from the governors of the school trust for just £8,500. One of the governors—Ambrose Congreve—objected to the sale and claimed that the building was worth £30,000.

A 113-year link was severed in November 1969 when the Clyde Shipping Company decided to terminate services on the Waterford–Liverpool route. Waterford Health Authority passed a provisional estimate in the final days of 1969 for its gross expenditure on health services in the city and county during 1970. The sum set aside—just over £2 million.

The 1970s

Flavours of the 1970s

Waterford in the 1970s was a city of optimism, even if there were dark clouds on the horizon as the Troubles in the North escalated. In 1972, following the Bloody Sunday killings, 18,000 marched in protest at the shootings by the British Army of unarmed civilians. Employers allowed employees off work to march. The front page of the *Munster Express* had a black border with the main news story on it, plus photos of the demonstration and speakers.

This was the largest demonstration since the Home Rule one in 1914, 68 years earlier. Deputy Mayor Tom Brennan spoke, and councillors, trade unions and chambers of commerce were represented. Near the platform some IRA local volunteers, Provisional and Official, fired volleys of gunfire at the end of the speeches, catching the dignitaries by surprise. The Last Post was played before the crowds dispersed. Twenty teenagers were brought to hospital after a builders' scaffold on which people had climbed to hear speeches, collapsed.

New car for £900

A new car model was launched in the course of 1970 at Scanlon's Garage on Hanover Street. The Avenger was available for less than £900. Other motoring bargains on offer included a one-year-old four-door Ford Cortina with bucket seats that was available for £795. It was confirmed during 1970 that work would begin before the year ended on the proposed Shopping Centre in Lisduggan. It was expected to take 18 months to complete and cost £200,000.

Advertising booms

The *Munster Express* was now up to 20 and 22 pages, advertising was more buoyant and large adverts prevailed. Hearnes Drapers of the Quay had a big autumn sale.

The Christmas edition was crammed with ads with the supplement rising to 48 pages, twice the normal amount. In October 1971 there was a big page ad for McInerney Homes for their houses in Lismore Park, Lismore Lawn, close to the Waterford Crystal plant in Kilbarry and the IDA Industrial Estate. It proved very popular and sold well.

The roof fell in

March of 1970 saw gardaí refuse to work at the South Parade station in Waterford where the ceiling in the day room had fallen in. The law enforcers had to conduct their enquiries from an adjoining bicycle shed!

Gun-running in Waterford

Waterford had its own gun-running incident, when in 1973 the ship, the *Claudia*, was arrested outside Helvick Head near Ring. Three Co. Waterford men were arrested, one mid county teacher and another two from Dungarvan. The 298-ton ship had come to Co. Waterford via Libya, Tunis and Cadiz in Spain, carrying several tons of arms and explosives on board destined for Northern Ireland. An Irish naval minesweeper intercepted the ship and the arms were later landed in Cobh by the authorities. Inspector Murtagh of Waterford was one of the investigating gardaí.

First day at school, Ferrybank National School

The air strip

The air strip was still an issue back in early 1972. The South East Regional Development Company was looking at new locations for an air strip, a decade or so later they would plump for Killowen, on the way to Dunmore East, with Waterford City Manager, Michael Doody authorising the land purchase.

Multi channel TV

Television reception of anything but RTÉ was unreliable in the 1970s, depending on good high pressure weather in the summer to get BBC in black and white. Some houses had large masts to get the signal.

Val Doonican being honoured at City Hall with his wife Lynn and Mayor Tim Galvin

D. Walsh, an enthusiast from Ballyneale, Carrick, who had good technical knowledge, led a campaign to get multi channel to the south east such as Dublin enjoyed.

Mick Browne's *Munster Express* 'Video Views' column was a great supporter. At the end of 1972, the Minister for Posts and Telegraphs, Gerry Collins, in a statement to the *Munster Express* stated that a new transmitter in South West Wales would supply the south east with colour BBC1 and BBC2 plus Harlech TV from Wales. Mr Walsh disagreed with the Minister, saying that the signal might reach parts of Wexford consistently but not Waterford. It seemed a change of the law on re-transmission would be needed.

The *Munster Express* and Mick Browne led this campaign, with public meetings. There was some opposition, particularly from RTÉ and Irish language enthusiasts.

RTÉ would lose advertising audiences and its monopoly but most would see the advantage in the end. Eventually, the law was changed and a Canadian company under the name Marlin and Phoenix came to Waterford to provide the British channels. In 1975 Marlin Cablevision announced that Tramore and New Ross would not be served by the new system due to insufficient household size. These towns had to wait more than another decade and a half for MMDS and satellite TV with Sky. The arrival of Sky television in the 1990s made the channel choice even greater with dozens of channels in various languages becoming available.

Judge McCay

One of the most famous local judges of the 1970s was Hedley McCay. Known as Deadly Hedley, he came on the scene when crime had begun to rise. Criminals feared the judge as he showed little tolerance and had no hesitation in sending them to jail. A good friend of Editor J. J. Walsh, he obliged him many a time with a great headline that in turn sold lots of newspapers, as the public of Waterford, both country and city would read up on the criminals' latest escapades. In 1979 the newspaper reported the judge's death aged just 54 years. He was born in Buttevant, Cork, and studied at Queen's University, King's Inns and the Sorbonne in Paris. He spoke French, German and Dutch. A great judge, tough but fair.

New garda station

Earlier in the century there were several small police stations in Waterford, numbering seven before 1920, but in the 1970s there was no full-time garda station. The newspaper campaigned for a new garda station as the guards were shifted to various places like South Parade and Newtown in the 1970s. After much lobbying, they were provided with good facilities in Ballybricken.

Taoiseach Jack Lynch with Councillor Joe Cummins. On Mr Lynch's right is Denis Keating a former director of Waterford FC.

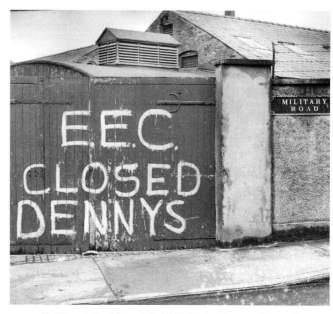

Public opinion blamed the EEC for the closure of Denny's

Tourism in Tramore

The Grand Hotel Tramore was sold in 1973 to the Cusack brothers; Arthur worked for Breen Hotels as general manager, his brother Michael was with South East Tourism.

Jim Tuohy came from Mosney in Meath to run Tramore Fáilte, and the amusement park, boating lake, putting greens and many other attractions. Visitor numbers jumped in Tramore as the good times hit Ireland.

Tramore Golf Club also expanded, to become one of the top 20 golf courses in the UK and Ireland with an excellent clubhouse, part funded by Bord Fáilte.

In the early part of the decade, Dublin, inland Irish and UK visitors flocked to Tramore, although the numbers of English tourists would lessen because of the Northern troubles.

1972 General Election—Fine Gael-Labour coalition elected

Waterford played a key role in the election with Fianna Fáil losing a seat to Labour's Tom Kyne in Dungarvan. This extra seat would play a pivotal role in delivering a mere four-seat majority for the Fine Gael-Labour coalition. Tom was a full-time trade union official and was aged 69 years when he regained the seat lost at a previous election.

Fad Browne of Fianna Fáil topped the poll. Across the river in Carlow-Kilkenny, Kieran Crotty of Fine Gael was the poll-topper with the Fianna Fáil Minister for Defence, Jim Gibbons second. Gibbons had been very badly treated by the Haughey faction in Fianna Fáil over his evidence and role in the Arms Crisis.

As a former Agriculture Minister Gibbons was credited with assisting dairy giant Avonmore to expand and with the successful development of Kildalton College, Piltown, Co. Kilkenny, as an Agricultural Training College.

Industry

The entry of Ireland to the EEC in 1972 threatened some local jobs. Clover Meats factory workers demonstrated against the live export of cattle and sheep to Italy by the Clyde Shipping Company. The *Munster Express* published a photo of a coffin, symbolising the loss of Clover jobs if this continued. Dennys Meats did close later in this decade with jobs going to Limerick.

The jute textiles factory closed during the decade also. Over 1,000 local jobs went in the early years as the industry structure changed. Waterford Crystal, however, was set to expand.

Following entry into the EEC, American firms increasingly came to see Ireland as a base for exports to member states. One example was the firm Camp Trails which made haversacks for back packers, for export to Holland and Germany. The firm expanded rapidly, from 64 to 100 jobs.

In 1975 Ulick O'Connor, a well known panellist on the RTÉ *Late Late Show* became a columnist in the newspaper, writing a Dublin sort of gossip column. He wrote on a wide variety of topics from apartheid politics in South Africa and how to control drinking, to an attack on the then current fashion of platform shoes. Sometimes controversial, the column was a change from the usual regional topics.

Leading members of the Clover Meats Ltd., Protest Parade, carry a coffin down Waterford Quay, on Wednesday last.

Clover Meats' workers in protest march

The march was in protest against the shipment of live cattle from Ireland, and as the workers held their demonstration, Gardai sealed off the Clyde Shipping Company's jetty where the M.V. Estancia was berthed, awaiting the loading of about 700 live cattle and 600 live sheep for Italy.

Production at the Waterford factory of Clover Meats Ltd., was disrupted for about two hours on Wednesday morning when over 500 employees stopped work and marched in a body through the city's main shopping centre.

The workers, some of them carrying placards, bearing slogans such as: "We want work, not words", "exporting cattle means exporting jobs", and "Will the Minister save our hides?", paraded from Christendom and along the Waterford quays, The Mall, Parnell Street, through John St., Michael Street, Broad Street, and Barronstrand Street, on to the quays again and back to the factory. Workers at the head of the parade carried a mock black coffin inscribed with the words "Clover Meats Jobs, R.I.P."

REDUNDANCIES

The workers are members of the I.T.&.WU., and the secretary of Waterford No. 1 branch of the union, Mr. John Dwan said on Wednesday that the protest march was organised in order to focus attention on the grave danger to employment in the fresh meat industry nationally, due to

Minister and the employers concerned in order to discuss the long term and short term prospects for the industry.

"The action taken by the Clover Meats workers is not directed at the Company, but at the delay and seeming reluctance of those responsible to take the urgent action required by the situation.

"It does not make sense to the workers concerned that the raw material on which they and their families depend for their livelihood, should be shipped out of the port of Waterford and other ports, to provide employment for workers in other countries. If the situation makes sense to those responsible for employment and for the planning of the economy, let this be demonstrated to the workers. If the situation does not make sense then it must be rectified immediately."

CRUELTY ALLEGED

The shipment of live cattle has already had a serious effect on a new Waterford factory, that of Messrs. R. & H. Wilson, Ltd., at Rathcullithem. During the summer, the management had to lay off 50 men because they were unable to obtain sufficient bones for conversion into collagen, for which the company had secured large orders on the continent.

The Waterford branch of the I.S.P.C.A. have been keeping a close watch on the shipment of live cattle and sheep through waterford It is claimed that in stormy weather, these in particular go through a severe time during the ship's voyage, and because of this, the Society had become concerned in the matter, a spokesman told The Munster Express on Wednesday.

the meat trades, but also in the tanning and other ancillary industries."

"The I.T.&.G.W.U." the statement went on, "have made continuous representations to the Minister for Agriculture over the past few years, and are now pressing for an early meeting with the

DRUNK-DRIVING CASE FAILS

Tramore District Court, on Tuesday, was told that it was not possible to have an independent analysis of a blood sample carried out anywhere in the Republic.

A medical witness in a alleged drunken-driving case said a pathologist colleague gave him this information.

The case before the court was his pocket. Then he took out a £1 one in which David Molloy, a 29-year-old butcher and farmer, of 2 Patrick Street, Tramore, was charged that he drove while drunk at Summerhill, Tramore, in the early hours of last Christmas morning.

Replying to Garda Supt. M. Sills,

arrived there at 1.15 a.m. and found the defendant content and his co-ordination was good. He was quite agitated, which was natural for a man in his position at that time, Te defendant was concerned about the interpretation of the Act. According to the Act witness should have been present when Dr. Twomey was carrying out his test, and it was on this point that the defendant was concerned. He had read the Act carefully and this was the purpose of his argument.

NO RE-CHECK

Dr. O'Brien-Moran who had earlier mentioned that this was the first case under the new Act

FOOT AND MOUTH DISEASE PRECAUTIONS

Because of the outbreak of Foot and Mouth Disease in England the Department of Agriculture and Fisheries is intensifying the measures permanently in operation to protect this country from the disease.

One of these measures is the restriction on the Movement of Persons) Order, 1968 which provides that any person coming to this country from Great Britain

WANT CERTIFICATE WITHDRAWN FROM BOOKMAKER

In a High Court case in Dublin on Monday two County Wicklow men declared their intention of suing Garda Superintendent Matthew Sills of Tramore, and Mrs. Dorothy Power, The Cross, Tramore, the latter

Letters to the Editor

Sinn Fein, Cumann James Connolly, Portlairge.
113, An Ce.
Portlairge.
11th December, 1972.

Northern Ireland C.R.A. Dependants' Fund

A Chara,

As you probably are aware the above organisation, last year, initiated a collection in Waterford

New Ross Notes

The New Ross Junior Chamber's annual dinner dance, was held in the Five Counties Hotel on Friday, December 8th was most successful, with music by the Alpines. The guest speaker was Mr. F. Zee, Managing Director of Albatros Fertilizers Ltd., New Ross.

Mr. Gerald Donovan N.T. P.C., New Ross was re-elected director at the election of Directors of South East Tourism at the recent annual meeting in Carlow. Mr. Donovan sought re-election as a nominee of local authorities contributing under £500 to the com-

Page Two · The Munster Express · Friday, 15th December, 1972

Road-side trading

The troubles in the North had opened up smuggling routes from Newry and elsewhere. At the time VAT, which of course the traders did not pay, was 19 per cent. With the currency difference, this meant that articles bought at the road-side could be 30 per cent cheaper than in the shops. Goods were purchased in the North and road-side traders sold them ex VAT, but with no guarantee. Televisions, other electrical goods, carpets, furniture were all sold in this way, much to the annoyance of legitimate traders paying rates and taxes.

In 1975 the matter was raised at a SERDO meeting by Tom Byrne of Wexford, who felt emergency powers should be brought in to stamp it out. Eventually, Customs and the Gardaí were brought into action as well as the Revenue because so much VAT revenue was lost.

Summer stories

The long hot summer of 1976 caused the local reservoirs to almost run dry. Water rationing had to take place in the Tramore area with local reservoirs Carrigavantry and Ballyscanlon in bad shape. Another summer story was that access to the Metal Man was cut off. Too many people had wanted to visit the beauty spot and hop three times around it, in response to the legend that you would marry within the year if you succeeded. Unfortunately, these romantic types damaged fences and the access was cut off and is still not accessible in 2010.

Woman living in shed

Another big story on the front page in the summer of 1976 was that of a woman aged 64 years, who lived in a shed, with no toilet or heat in winter. Mary Power lived in a coal shed 15 feet by 9 feet, eight and a half miles from Waterford near Ballyduff Lower. Dr A. Kelly reported this appalling state of affairs and Ald. Gallagher made a representation on her behalf.

Farmers attacked in farmhouse by burglars

Later in 1976, there was a court case report of a farmhouse raid on a house near Kill. The defendants were sentenced to three years penal servitude for robbery with violence and grievous bodily harm. They had robbed another house in the area also.

Snippets from other pages

In July 1976 the British Ambassador, Christopher Ewart Biggs, was killed by a land mine in Dublin. In a front page headline the *Munster Express* called it 'murder most foul'.

On a positive note, the Granville Hotel opened a new lounge in the same building where Thomas Francis Meagher, the initiator of the Irish Tricolour, was born and raised.

To end quickie marriages, and to forestall couples who were ill prepared, the Bishop of Waterford decreed new rules for church marriages, requiring the couples to be both over 18 years and to give three months notice of marriage.

Clover Meats were still struggling and had a share drive for more capital. Kilmeaden Cheese co-op expanded as the EEC paid large sums for farmer produce. The co-op held special open days.

Gay Byrne promoted RTV rental TVs in adverts, L and N and Quinnsworth had huge adverts in paper in the run up to Christmas.

Ken Barry, father of magician Keith, a Tops of the Town man, played for the Concorde Musical band in Passage East, or as the *Munster Express* paper put it, he zoomed into Passage.

Noel Griffin, centre with pen, signing another important contract for Waterford Crystal

Industry news

The Ross Shipyard in New Ross, which employed 400, expanded with new oil rig deck orders. The booming oil industry in the North Sea , Kinsale Gas Field and elsewhere would be a great stimulus for Ross increasing employment.

Waterford Crystal expanded in the late 1970s, with ever-rising profits. They were up 42 per cent to £4.7m and more jobs were created there.

The troubles at Munster Chipboard and other traditional industries continued. In 1979 there was a takeover of the troubled chipboard factory. There had been calls for nationalisation as it was a strategic industry harnessing the natural resource, wood. This had happened in the Fianna Fáil stronghold of Clare but it was not to be in Waterford.

In 1979 Brian Lenihan promised to re-open the plant and there was an agreement with the ATGWU and the city manager to get the factory up and running again in what was an interim progressive move.

There had been disputes also at the paper mills with a massive demonstration for jobs in 1978, with 15,000 workers marching for government help to save local traditional industries or replace them with IDA-backed new ones. There were protests to RTÉ about lack of TV coverage of some of the marches and lack of concern for Waterford's plight.

Hearnes department stores was closed and sold with Granville.

TV signals threatened

A big concern on the front page was the threat to shut off Waterford Cablevision due to re-broadcasting of signals from Minaun Cheekpoint to Waterford.

Mayor Tim Galvin (centre) at the opening of the playground in St John's Park

War criminal in Waterford

Peter Menten of Holland, a war criminal, was resident in Comeragh House, Lemybrien, Co. Waterford. He had been sentenced for his part in the massacre of Jews in Holland during the Second World War. He had not long been released from jail in Holland and the British media had a regular watch to see would he come back to Ireland after the case.

Booming economy

New firms like Measurex, later known as Honeywell, would set up in Waterford and recruit heavily from the electronic courses in Waterford Regional Technical College. This would create new attractions for investment in Waterford.

By 1979 the general Irish economy was booming and after the Fianna Fáil pump priming of the economy, extra public service jobs were created in health, education and local authorities. To meet the new demand the *Munster Express* installed a new newspaper colour print unit allowing advertising in colour.

The year also saw Waterford reach an FAI soccer cup final; this time they would be beaten but would win the following year over St Pat's.

Workers' and other protests

The year 1979 saw more massive workers' marches in Waterford, this time for a fair system of taxation. Ten thousand marched down the Quay as businesses let staff off to go and march. Personal income taxes were high, with a marginal rate of 65 per cent, as the Waterford-born Minister for Economic Planning Dr Martin O'Donoghue, abolished rates on houses and tax on cars, but pushed up income tax rates. Because of the high marginal rates of tax it was often more attractive for single people to go on the dole, especially if they could get some black economy work.

The advertising market develops 1969/70

In the 1950s and 1960s local newspapers were a favoured way of promoting national brands, so local papers such as the *Munster Express* did well. And then RTÉ, launched in 1962, began to take much of that business. The paper's advertising people had now to look locally to fill the gap. Property, motors and jobs became and are still mainstays of the newspaper's advertising. Local retailers such as the department store, Shaws, or electrical firms like Furlongs, RTV Rentals or Thorn were other big advertisers.

Advertising features for small business became a new phenomenon and the *Munster Express* was quick to develop this. A hairdresser called Karl Casey, who was a relation of J. J.'s wife Josephine, came into the office to advertising manager Michael Whelan with the idea. He explained that he had recently seen in Dublin a promotion by a top hairdresser there consisting of a page of appropriate text with support ads. Karl's Hairdressers became the first Waterford business to do a fully illustrated advertising feature with support ads.

To develop this new idea an advertising executive was hired but he moved on, then the irrepressible Davy Daniels was recruited and he proved to be a great ad canvasser from 1972 till his retirement over three decades later. His popularity led him later to politics and he is current Deputy Mayor of Waterford. The paper's photographer Eoin Murphy proved to be a great colleague of Davy with his excellent creative photographs of businesses and people, offering a great service for advertisiers.

This revenue helped to make up for the national advertising decline with advertisements for national brands going to TV. Major advertisers such as Unilever for example, previously the top national advertiser in the *Munster Express,* moved their advertising spend from the regional press to the glamorous new medium of television.

Another area of growth was small ads. As Waterford grew there was a greater demand for rental property for people coming to seek work there. In Memoriams, with photos in black and white, were another feature.

Despite competition from other media, Waterford was still seen as an important market with strong industries like Waterford Crystal, Waterford Co-op and many international firms. National advertising remained at 15–20 per cent of the business.

Stephanie's

Stephanie's was a club in Tramore's Silver Slipper Ballroom run by Mike Kent. Mike brought some new and radically different bands to Stephanie's and is the man who organised a weekend in 1971 which is still talked about.

On that famous weekend, Mike brought Rory Gallagher, Thin Lizzy and Skid Row to the seaside venue. Of course, this wasn't Phil Lynott's first gig in Tramore, as he had previously played across the road in the Atlantic Ballroom in a relief band called The Black Eagles. Mike is also responsible for giving Horslips their first gig in the town when they played for a £50 fee.

Stephanies ran until 1973 when Mike turned his attention to Waterford and in particular the Ardree Hotel where he became entertainments manager. Mike introduced a very popular Saturday night scene with a combination of cabaret, disco and national band. The night would run from 8.30 pm to 1.30 am and all for £1. Local groups provided the cabaret—Dick & Mick, Jed & The Southern Express, Rocky & Nightlife, Charlie Matthews Band and Rory O'Connor Chapter. The bigger bands would follow the disco and finish the marathon session. Some of the bands who played there were Thin Lizzy, Big 8, Joe Dolan, The Bay City Rollers, Horslips, Mungo Gerry, The Dubliners, Brendan Grace, Tweed, the Miami Showband, Dickie Rock, Chips.

Rory Gallagher

Phil Lynott

"The Munster Express"
FRIDAY, FEBRUARY 4, 1972

has a GREATER CIRCULATION (net sales) than the TOTAL of All Waterford and Kilkenny 'papers

PALOMINO SHERRIES
Bottled in Spain
Dry - Medium - Cream

John Egan
WATERFORD

The Munster Express

(Incorporating "The Waterford Citizen," "The Celt" and "The Waterford Standard")

First Edition

Registered in the General Post Office as a Newspaper.

ESTABLISHED 1859 (112th YEAR)   FRIDAY, FEBRUARY 4, 1972

20 PAGES

(Express Delivery)
Britain, 6½p

PRICE 5p

PRICE 5p (Including Wholesale and Turnover Tax).

QUESTIONS
1—Name the charter which granted religious and political freedom to the French Huguenots in 1398?
2—What does the charge of homesucker mean in Scottish law?
3—When did the Republic of the Philippines come into existence?
4—Which game was invented by James Naismith?
(Answers at bottom of page)

WATERFORD MOURNS DERRY

BIGGEST DEMONSTRATION FOR ALMOST 60 YEARS

Waterford mourned the deaths of the victims of Sunday's tragic shootings in Derry by a massive public demonstration at Ballybricken Hill on Wednesday. Senior citizens — who were very young at the time — say, and the files of newspapers bear them out, that it was the biggest outdoor gathering of it's kind held in Waterford since a Sunday in January in 1914 when a monster national demonstration was organised to strengthen Ireland's case for Home Rule, which was passed and put on the Statute Book but never executed. At that time the city was preparing for weeks in advance with the decoration of buildings with flags, evergreens etc. There was one big difference, in that Wednesday's demonstration was a spontaneous one and was not confined to any particular section and was held in the middle of the working week. Employers were imbued with the same sympathetic patriotic spirit and closed their factories and other premises to enable the workers to take part in the demonstration in which they too participated. Despite a gale, with heavy rain and strong winds, an established 18,000 turned out to show solidarity with the minority in the Six Counties; to demonstrate their abhorrence at Sunday's shootings and to express their sympathy with relatives of the bereaved. It was a most remarkable and memorable sight on the historic hill of Ballybricken at 4.15 when all the contingents had converged there and stood in the rain awaiting the arrival of the members of the City Council and officials of the Corporation, in their robes of office, headed by the Deputy Mayor of the city, Alderman Thomas Brennan.

A special platform was provided in front of Messrs. Breen's Better Value Supermarket, on which the Deputy Mayor, and Corporation members were joined by the Most Reverend Michael Russell, D.D., Bishop of Waterford and Lismore; the Rt. Reverend John Ward Armstrong, M.A., B.D., Church of Ireland Bishop of Cashel, Emly, Waterford and Lismore; the Reverend Fergus Day, Church of Ireland Dean of Waterford; the Reverend Dudley Cooney, Methodist Church; the Reverend S. Watt, Presbyterian Church; Mr. Maurice Wigham, Society of Friends; Mr. Luke O'Sullivan, President, Waterford Chamber of Commerce and Mr. Des Purcell, President, Waterford Junior Chamber.

FRIGHTENING OCCURRENCE

The proceedings included only one speech, given by the Deputy Mayor. About half-way through his address, there was a sensational and frightening occurrence when a 30-feet tubular scaffold, which had been erected against the Better Value Supermarket, collapsed under the weight of about 70 youths and girls. The scaffold had been placed against the building for the purpose of carrying out alterations and renovations to the premises, and it was not generally noticed that so many had clamoured to that point of vantage. Cries went up when it was seen to shake and finally sag. It was the sagging and the manner in which it fell — sideways, in jurics — that saved the lives of the youths and girls were said yesterday to be comas well as those underneath it and fortable.

REVOLVER VOLLEYS

When the demonstration proceedings were resumed, the Deputy Mayor called on the two Bishops to lead the gathering in the recitation of the Lord's Prayer. Immediately afterwards, revolver volleys were fired by a joint party from the Provisional and Official wings of the I.R.A. in the Waterford district, which had taken up a position close to the platform. The firing of the volleys took the gathering by surprise and many in the attendance were unaware of what precisely was happening.

A joint statement on behalf of both wings of the IRA was issued on Wednesday night stating that they had combined to form a joint firing party at the demonstration and that they had fired 12 revolver volleys. The demonstration was brought to a close by the sounding of the Last Post.

Afterwards, special Masses were offered up in Waterford Cathedral it was attended by Ald. Brennan, members of the City Council and Corporation officials; Ballybricken Church and Dominican Church. A combined Service for members of the Church of Ireland, Presbyterian and Methodist Churches and the Society of Friends, at which Ald. S. McClure represented the Mayor and Corporation, took place in Christ Church Cathedral.

Sign of solidarity in Kilkenny

Masses in all Kilkenny City Churches and Service in St. Canice's Protestant Cathedral marked Kilkenny's day of mourning on Wednesday for the victims of the Derry shootings.

All city business premises, factories and offices were closed from 1 a.m., and Tricolours were flown at half-mast from the City Hall and other public buildings. Outside the City Hall entrance, there was a black coffin draped in the Tricolour and black flags were flown from many city premises.

Employees of firms and business premises in the city marched in procession to Mass in St. Mary's Cathedral, which was celebrated by the Rev. J. Hoynes, C.C. The cathedral and, indeed, all the other churches were packed for the special Masses.

Rev. Father Hoynes said the Mass, for those who lost their lives and for the injured, as well as for the consolation of their families and relatives, was an expression of sympathy to them on behalf of the Bishop, priests and people of Kilkenny, and a sign of their solidarity with them in the struggle for civil rights which would enable them to give a life worthy of human dignity.

Attending Mass in the Cathedral was the Deputy Mayor, Mr. John Holohan; members of Kilkenny Corporation, and Mr. P. J. Treehan (Chairman) and members of Kilkenny Co. Council, Mayor Kieran Crotty, T.T., attended the funerals in Derry.

Rt. Rev. Dr. H. R. McAdoo, Protestant Bishop of Ossory, Ferns and Leighlin, presided at Intercession Service in St. Canice's Cathedral, at which the Very Rev. B. Harvey, Dean of Ossory, and the Rev. John Neill, Bishop's Vicar, officiated.

Kilkenny Corporation was represented at the Service by Miss

NO SERIOUS INJURIES

A number of youths standing on the top platform of the scaffold grabbed the parapet of the supermarket roof as the scaffold began to sag. One of them, however, lost his grip and came crashing down, receiving a broken ankle. Another person crashed through one of the pane glass windows in the store but he too was not seriously injured. It was quite some time before order was restored as parents tried to make their way towards the falling scaffold, fearing that their sons or daughters had been killed or injured.

About twenty of the teenagers were treated in Ardkeen Hospital, but only about nine were detained. Three of them, Pat Hayes (18½), Newport's Sq; Breda Power (14), Connolly Place, and Brigid Daunt (15), Hennessy's Rd., all suffering from shock, were kept in the Sacred Heart Unit, while the others, all youths, are being treated for various injuries — chest, shoulder and arm — in St. Teresa's Unit. All

Whilst the concourse of people assembled on Ballybricken Hill were awaiting the start of the proceedings, a number of youths venturously climbed on to scaffolding over the speakers' platform at the Besco Supermarket. Our staff photographer's camera caught this sequence. Top picture shows the scene seconds before the collapse when it appeared very dangerous. Bottom picture shows the youths clinging to the roof to save themselves from injury. The second from the left, actually fell to the ground amid cries from the huge crowd. It was feared at this juncture that injuries would be serious.

In Dungarvan

In Dungarvan business came to a standstill and an estimated 3,000 people took part in a march

Waterford represented

Sinn Fein statement

The Sinn Fein Regional Area Committee (Waterford/Wexford/Kilkenny) issued the following statement yesterday (Thursday):

"The shooting of Civil Rights Supporters in Derry last Sunday was another instance of British Imperial policy in the Commonwealth, these are the tactics of British imperialists as demonstrated in the era of Ghandi in India, the massacre in Sharpeville, and the atrocities in Ghana in an attempt to steamroll the people into political settlements in England's interest.

"We condemn the stern policy of the Dublin Government and the Opposition parties in standing 'idly by' while the British Army endeavour to enforce a military solution which involves internment without trial. The driving out from certain districts the men folk and youths and the intimidation of women and children.

"It is a tragedy that the shooting had to happen, to shake Leinster House into this reality. We demand that no talks be held with those who are pursuing this policy and it is obvious that there will be no peace in Ireland until internment ends and the British Army of occupation and British Imperialism are rooted forever.

"It was decided at a special meeting of the above committee to send Sean Walsh to represent the region at the funerals in Derry and to confer with local Republicans on all aspects of the situation there.

"At the meeting it was decided to take up collections on behalf of Derry I.R.A. Units and to hold public meetings.

"A special meeting on the present situation is being held by the Kilkenny Comhairle Ceanntair of Sinn Fein and the local cumanns in Waterford City on Tuesday last."

WORKERS' RESOLUTION

At the weekly meeting of the Waterford Combined Factories Social Club, a resolution was passed strongly condemning the murderous action of the British forces in Derry on Sunday.

A further resolution, agreeing fully with the Taoiseach's statements on the Northern situation, was passed unanimously.

Personality Portrait

British troops that they were attacked by snipers. I wonder and I

The staff on the Tramore bus route which replaced the train

Waterford Regional Technical College opens

Waterford's population stood at 29,462 in January 1968, up 5.1 per cent since 1961.In June 1968 Minister for Education, Brian Lenihan TD (father of the later Minister for Finance), announced 'a very important step' in Irish technical education—the signing of contracts for the first three (Carlow, Dundalk and Waterford) of nine regional technical colleges.

Minister Lenihan said the colleges would not be just technical schools but would each have a 'top' subject taught to a university degree level. Each college would cost about £540,000 and have a capacity of 1,000 students. The scheme as a whole had originally been conceived by Dr Paddy Hillery when he was Minister for Education and would cost a grand total of £7m.

The new colleges, Mr Lenihan said, would be growth centres in the full social and economic sense, and poles of attraction for all kinds of development. He added: 'The main long-term function of the colleges will be to educate for trade and industry over a broad spectrum of occupations ranging from craft to professional level, notably in engineering and science, including agriculture, but also in commercial, linguistic, catering, art and design, and other specialities.'

On 12 December 1968 Minister Lenihan told the Dáil that, while the initial estimate for the cost of Waterford Regional Technical College had been £790,000, the expected spend had fallen to £660,000 on foot of detailed design and cost studies carried out by Building Design Associates working with his Department officials.

In July 1969, a joint recruitment ad for principals at the regional technical colleges in Athlone, Sligo, Carlow, Dundalk and Waterford ran in Irish and British print media simultaneously. Candidates were required to have a university degree in science (honours); commerce (honours); agricultural science; architecture; engineering or an approved equivalent as well as five or more years experience in research, industry or teaching. The salary for married men was IR£2,580, rising to £3,000 with six £70 increments. Women and single men would be paid £2,200–2,500. For context, £3,600 was the cost of a three-bedroom, semi-detached McInerney Construction house with garage and fuel store at Lismore Lawn for handover in early 1971.

Twenty-four teachers would be required to staff the Waterford Regional Technical College in September to provide instructors for the courses proposed for 1970/71. Teachers would be needed for general subjects; science and mathematics; commerce and business studies; woodwork and building construction; electrical installation; physical education; religion and civil, electrical and mechanical engineering.

The Irish Times of 15 May 1970 carried a report headed 'THE NEW COLLEGES' ROLE' on a speech by Jerry Sheehan, senior inspector, Department of Education, in which he examined the context and challenges of the new regional technical colleges. On student recruitment, he said four things were needed to attract students to the colleges. These were a range of interesting studies with career opportunities, vertical mobility in higher institutions, proper student aid and a widely accepted status for qualifications. 'All in all, a fairly tall order, which, I believe nevertheless, is within our national capacity to fill.' Mr Sheehan also said he felt that industry should now be expected to spell out, more explicitly than it had to date, the skills it wanted, so the colleges could work to meet them. This was more difficult than it sounded, as educationalists did not always speak the same language as industrialists.

On 31 July 1970, Waterford Regional Technical College—the second in a series around the country, costing £5.5m—was formally handed over by contractors Mahon & McPhillips Ltd of Kilkenny to the Minister for Education. Minister Pádraig Faulkner said at the handover ceremony that it was no accident that Waterford was chosen to have one of the colleges as there were many industries which had established themselves in the city and the Government had plans for it to develop as a major growth centre. Industry, he said, needed a supply of trained and qualified people to ensure its successful growth.

The new Waterford Regional Technical College was due to formally open its doors to students on 22 September 1970 having had students in temporary accommodation from a year earlier. The first college principal was Richard Langford BA BComm. HDip., a native of Birr, Co. Offaly who was to remain until 1974 when he became CEO of the City of Waterford Vocational Education Committee.

It was anticipated that 80–100 scholarships would be available for third level courses by 1971–2. The first ever meeting of the Council of Waterford's new regional technical college elected the Bishop's representative Right Rev. Monsignor Dean Michael Barron, PP, as chairman. Dean Barron was unanimously elected having been proposed by Larry White, President, Waterford Council of Trade Unions. Other Waterford representation on the original college Council included Eddie Collins TD.

The Irish Times on 6 February 1971 included an analysis by education correspondent Michael Heney of the rollout of the regional technical colleges. He noted how the beginnings of the Regional Technical Colleges were 'buried somewhere' in a Cabinet meeting before 20 September 1966 when the Steering Committee on Technical Education was set up after the decision had been made to locate colleges at Cork, Limerick, Waterford, Galway, Sligo, Dundalk, Athlone and Carlow with the committee—chaired by Noel Mulcahy, Irish Management Institute—to advise on a potential college which ultimately proceeded in Letterkenny. Their findings were presented to the Department of Education in April 1967.

The range of courses proposed for the college can be seen from a recruitment advertisement in *The Irish Times* for teaching posts in electrical/electronics engineering; biology; chemistry; mathematics; chartered accounting; costs and works accounting; law and commerce/economics. A further round of vacancies existed for teachers of metalwork; woodwork and building construction; physical education; commerce with shorthand and typewriting; commerce with general subjects; general subjects (including Irish, English, History, Geography) and a careers counsellor.

In 1979 the WRTC began to provide degree courses, and in 1998 it was the first to be awarded Institute of Technology status. The Institute was granted delegated authority by the National Council for Educational Awards to confer its own certificates and diplomas, and now issues awards at all levels from Higher Certificate to PhD. Now, forty years later, Waterford Institute of Technology is one of Ireland's leading higher education institutions with more than 10,000 students and 1,000 staff.

Left hook floored Fianna Fáil Mayoralty *by* TOM YOUNG

In 1974 the *Munster Express* had two of its staff elected to Waterford City Council which was a source of pride within a company which employed fewer than forty full-time workers. Not only were Davy Daniels and Paddy Gallagher voted onto the local authority at first time of asking, but they each secured such support that they were among the Council's aldermen, an honour reserved for the biggest vote-catchers.

It can be said that both of them made a major impression over a long number of years in public life. Davy, an Independent still going strong as Father of the current Council, topped the poll in virtually all subsequent elections, and Paddy, a Dáil deputy for eight months in 1982, continued as a councillor until 1999 when he retired to concentrate on production of his own newspaper.

Paddy regularly made the news himself in his early years on the Council. He quickly developed a reputation as something of a political Rottweiler, representing what would have been seen as the hard-left doctrine of Sinn Féin The Workers Party.

Munster Express staff make a presentation to their colleague Alderman Davy Daniels when he became Mayor
Back row (l–r) Pierce Dower, Michael O'Keeffe, Paul Hutchinson, Joe Dalton, Dermot Blount, Willie Hennessy, Tony Rogers, Mick Browne, Des Hodge, Michael Whelan, Jack Williams
Front row (l–r) Tom Young, John O'Connor, Jack Kennedy, Mayor Davy Daniels, Teddy Barry, Frank Walsh, Kieran Walsh (Photo Eoin Murphy)

The Mayoral election of 1979 provided an example of his determination to fight his corner and that of his party. It had already become clear that its members—Davy Walsh had joined him on the Council at that stage—stood no chance of getting elected Mayor because of policies which differed drastically to those of the mainstream parties, Fianna Fáil, Fine Gael and Labour.

Mayors were always elected by securing a majority vote through pre-agreements, often finalised in the final minutes before the election procedure. These pacts never included representatives of Sinn Féin The Workers (SFWP) Party, later to become known as just the Workers Party. Nonetheless, this method of choosing the Mayor had never been considered controversial until Paddy and Davy Walsh started highlighting what they saw as the injustice of such pacts depriving them of the honour of serving as Mayor.

So Paddy Gallagher and Davy Walsh decided with their party organisation in 1979 to have a meaningful input into the election, albeit a mischievous one. It was known in advance that the two candidates, Stephen Rogers of Fine Gael and Fianna Fáil's Joe Cummins, would be running neck and neck for the post. The SFWP team's first step was to ensure that the two finished level in terms of votes from the 15-strong Council.

It was decided that Davy Walsh would vote for his fellow Ferrybank councillor, Joe Cummins, bringing to seven his number of supporters. It was apparent in advance that Stephen Rogers would also garner seven votes, including that of his neighbour Davy Daniels, which would leave Paddy Gallagher with the casting vote.

On the night, with Davy Walsh having cast his vote, it was assumed within the Fianna Fáil grouping that Paddy, particularly given his republican background, would also support Joe, assuring him of success.

But that was to reckon without the left hook devised to floor Fianna Fáil's plans. Joe Cummins was in the process of rising to acknowledge victory when Paddy delivered a

Paddy Donegan Fine Gael Minister for Defence inspecting troops on parade at the Waterford City barracks, since closed

Josephine McCormack

McCormack's Hardware, Summerhill, Tramore

Eamon McCormack of McCormack's Hardware

Marie Fleming

hammer blow—he abstained. That left the decision to be made by means of a draw from a hat, with the Law Adviser of the time, Ian Farrell, doing the honours.

To the delight of Stephen Rogers, his name was the one that came out and so he was the one who donned the Mayoral robe and chain. Paddy Gallagher had made his point.

Water rates controversy

The imposition of water rates in Waterford City has long been a bone of contention. It has always been viewed as double taxation.

In 1977 Fianna Fáil swept to power nationally on the basis of removal of domestic rates. The shortfall to the Exchequer was filled by increasing VAT and income tax. To replace rates in paying for local services, the new government committed itself to a 100 per cent block grant to run the city.

In 1982 the Fine Gael-Labour coalition attempted to row back on this by cutting the block grant by 12 per cent. This created a shortfall in local authority finances throughout the country and the Minister for the Environment Dick Spring instructed councils to make up the shortfall by the imposition of a water tax. Waterford City Council, through a motion proposed by Councillor Davy Walsh of the Workers Party, at first decided to resist this new charge.

The following year this decision was reversed, and water rates were adopted by the City Council on a vote of 8 to 7. This caused a great amount of debate in Waterford. The combined residents' associations organized and picketed council meetings and councillors' homes. They demonstrated in the streets against this alleged unfair taxation.

To enforce their decision, the Council began to employ outside contractors to cut off the water supply to homes which would not pay assessed water charges. This was severely resisted by the combined residents' association and the Workers Party and resulted in two major sieges in Hillview, Waterford and in Paddy Brown Road, where the contractors were surrounded by activists who refused to let them depart the scene. Non-compliant tenants who had had their water cut off had it restored by activists.

The protests persuaded the Council to abandon the use of outside contractors. They then changed tack and proposed service charges for refuse collection. This was just as controversial, and twice in the following decade the City Council refused to pass the annual rates with service charges included. They were duly threatened with the imposition of a commissioner to run the city, and twice adopted the rates only at the 11th hour.

The one constant in the debate was the stance of the Workers Party who were implacably opposed to what they stigmatised as double taxation. They have paid considerably for this principled stand, in that they were denied elevation to the office of Mayor, and kept off important committees, such as the Harbour Board, the Airport, Health Committees, Chairs of SPC's, and the Health Forum. The Workers Party and their successors have had a constant presence on Waterford City Council from 1974 to this day.

Waterford's twin town

by DAVID WALSH

In 1979 a delegation of four people from St Herblain in Brittany came to Waterford to initiate talks about twinning. Leading the delegation were Christian Pellen, an old friend from the United Democratice Breton Party, Roland Paveageau, councillor in the Socialist Party, Renée Paulay, councillor in the Socialist Party, and Giselle

Augeareau, councillor in the Communist Party. They met with the Waterford City Manager, Micheal Doody, and several of the councillors. They presented a history of their city and stated that they were seeking to twin with an Irish city of similar size and history.

St Herblain is a suburb of Nantes which has a long history of trading with Waterford. In fact, after the Battle of the Boyne, King James was transported from the city of Waterford to Nantes. There was a lot of trade between Nantes and Waterford, in the line of Newfoundland flounder and wine and pork. Initially, Waterford City Council were reluctant to get involved in this twinning arrangement but the enthusiasm of Michael Doody and the drive of Councillor Davy Walsh cemented the relationship between the two cities. In May of 1982, a delegation from Waterford, led by Councillor Tom Brown, signed the twinning charter in St Herblain, and in October of that year a delegation led by Jean-Marc Ayerau, Mayor of St Herblain, signed the twinning charter in Waterford. The framed charter is on permanent display in City Hall. Little did we think that thousands of diverse exchanges between athletes, gymnasts, cyclists, bands, schools, adult education classes, dancers, active retired, sporting, youth workers, choral societies, would emanate from that beginning. As a public manifestation of the twinning, every year since 1980 delegates from St Herblain have participated in our St Patrick's Day Parade.

The twinning in the 1990s established contact between businesses in Waterford and St Herblain with a view to mutual networking, a situation that pertains until this day. Nantes Trade Fair attracted exhibits from 160 countries worldwide and we are proud to say that Waterford firms, e.g. Waterford Crystal, and tourism participated a number of times. Since its inception, the twinning endeavour has been at all times to make the arrangement inclusive. This twinning belongs to the people, it is about people meeting people with similar interests and its survival and progress from strength to strength is a testament to that fact.

A 30-member trade delegation came to Waterford three years ago for a seminar in City Hall for participants from the IDA, the Chamber of Commerce, the South Eastern Regional Authority and Bord Fáilte. Out of that seminar came participation from Waterford traders in the Christmas Fair in Nantes where successful trade was established. This trade mission was sponsored by the Waterford Enterprise Board. When Waterford played Bordeaux in the European Cup Winners Cup the city of St Herblain hosted Waterford United overnight on the way to the match. The biggest delegation that ever came from St Herblain was in 1984 when 348 people came for St Patrick's Day in Waterford in two plane-loads, arriving into Cork Airport and met by a host of buses to bring them to the city.

Another visit of note was when the Tour de France came to Waterford in 1998. A large delegation led by the Mayor, Charles Gautier, attended. They were then brought to the Munster Final in Thurles where Waterford played Clare to a draw; the match was thoroughly enjoyed by all the visitors. The 5th, 10th, 15th, 20th and 25th years of the twinning, have been celebrated, ending with a toast to the continuation of the twinning.

The town-twinning committee is indebted to the loyal members who have served (voluntarily) over a long period, in particular: Anthony McElroy, Jane Power, Liam Murphy, John Waters. The present committee consists of Councillor Davy Walsh, Chair, Eamonn Murphy, Secretary, Kieran Walsh, PRO, Philip Flynn, Treasurer, Anthony, Glendon, Vincent Walsh and Francis O'Neill.

The 1980s

The 1980s—A decade of political change and turbulence

The 1980s saw a change in economic conditions from boom to recession. Politically, the Northern troubles were still leaving people dead though fewer were being killed than during the early 1970s. Political instability in the south, with Fianna Fáil unable to get a working majority, caused three elections between June 1981 and November 1982, and more in 1987 and 1989. Elections were often good for newspapers with advertising by political parties, and a public eager for local news on the campaign.

Tramore Racecourse concerns
The year 1980 opened with a concern over the future of Tramore Racecourse which was up for sale and was applying for planning permission for housing. Cllrs Tom Healy and Con Casey opposed the planning change, but it was later granted. Since the housing slump in the 1980s meant little demand for development land, racing would continue until a takeover a decade later by a local group acquiring the Fleming family interests.

Bausch and Lomb come to the city
In 1980 Des O'Malley, Fianna Fáil Minister for Industry, came to Waterford to announce the opening of a great new industry in Waterford. The lens manufacturer Bausch and Lomb of Rochester, New York State, were going to get an advance factory of 45,000 square feet from the IDA on their industrial estate in Waterford. An initial £5m investment created 53 jobs; this rose to 300 and then 1,000 after five years in the manufacture of contact lenses. The company had pioneered the soft contact lens in 1971. Bausch and Lomb remains the largest employer in Waterford in 2010.

Industrial employment
In 1980, 2,300 people were employed in 1980 at the IDA Industrial Estate. With over 3,000 in Waterford Crystal, the city was a magnet for industrial employment. That year was a declining one for glass, with profits showing the first drop in many years.

Teenage drinking
The problem of teenage drinking reared its head on the front page; a 17-year-old was found drunk and incapable on Turkey Road, as the judge condemned the issuing of more licensing extensions.

New runway
Construction began on the new airport runway at Killowen. On the front page of the *Munster Express* in July 1981 a picture of a Cement Roadstone earth mover marked the commencement. The runway was finished later that autumn.

Politics darkened by North and Clover crisis
The 1981 H-Block hunger strikes and ongoing troubles at Clover Meats were key election topics in Waterford, with a large bearing on elections. In the June election Austin Deasy, later Minster for Agriculture, topped the poll in Waterford with 8,625 first preference votes, Jackie Fahy

The Munster Express

JET SHERIDAN OIL DISTRIBUTORS WATERFORD 'Phone: 051/72891 | Tractor Diesel: Motor Diesel Heating Oils | *It will pay you to contact us!*

FIRST EDITION 28 PAGES *Incorporating "The Waterford Citizen," "The Celt" and "The Waterford Standard."* EXPRESS DELIVERY BRITAIN 30p.

FREE FILM With any film developed and printed at **MULLIGANS CAMERA CENTRE** 39, BARRONSTRAND STREET

Registered at the General Post Office as a Newspaper | 122nd YEAR | Friday, 5th June, 1981 | PRICE: 25p including Value Added Tax.

450 NEW JOBS

Minister for Industry and Commerce, Mr. Des O'Malley was in Waterford on Wednesday with a promise of 450 new jobs divided between the city and Carrick-on-Suir.

At a Press Conference in the Ardree Hotel he announced that the IDA had concluded negotiations with three companies for the location of a new manufacturing project in Carrick (Rexnord Inc.) and the expansion of two existing operations, (Kromberg and Schubert Ireland Ltd and Garrett Ireland Ltd.), on Waterford's Industrial Estate.

The total job target, at full production, is "almost 450." Rexnord Inc. of Wisconson a billion dollar manufacturer of engineering equipment, already has a facility in Athlone, set up last year. The Carrick project will involve a total investment of nearly £5 million in premises, plant and machinery. The company plans to create employment for 330 persons at full production. Rexnord will acquire the IDA's 27,000 sq. ft. advance factory on an eight acre site at Carrick and initial production is expected to get underway in the next few months.

The new project will involve the manufacture of the company's camloc quarter turn fasteners and tension latches which are used for quick release of access panels in the aircraft

programme first announced in 1978. The company plans to increase its investment by a further £4 million which will bring the company's total investment in Waterford to £3.5 million. The new expansion programme involves the construction of a 24,000 sq. ft. extension to the company's existing factory and the purchase of additional specialised machinery. An additional 51 jobs are expected to be created as a result of this investment - this will bring the total employment at the company in

exported through the port of Waterford to customers in the U.K. and in Continental Europe.

The second company to expand its operations in Waterford is Garrett Ireland Ltd., which has finalised negotiations with the I.D.A. for a revision to its investment

NEW OFFICES

Councillor William Kenneally, T.D. has been informed by the Minister of State at the Department of Finance, Mr. Tom McEllistrim, that Bell's old premises at Exchange Street, Waterford will be demolished and on the site will be built a

EXPANSIONS

Kromberg and Schubert has committed itself to a further investment of almost £.75 million at its Waterford plant which will involve the creation of an additional 66 new jobs. This will bring to almost 400 the number of persons who will be employed by the company in

Waterford plant to 187 over the next four years.

Garrett Ireland Ltd., occupies a 24,000 sq. ft. factory on a five acre site on the Waterford Industrial Estate, where it began production of aluminium castings for the aircraft and automotive industry in 1979. The company employs 42 persons at present. The company's full order book, combined with its plans to introduce new products, indicate a bright future for the company.

TRAMORE TERROR

At last Tuesday night's meeting of Tramore Town Commissioners Mrs. Theresa Phelan complained about the incidents of violence and crime which occurred in the seaside resort over the Bank Holiday week-end. She also alleged that there were simply not enough Gardai on duty to deal with the amount of trouble.

She paid tribute to the men who were on duty and said they did the best they could under the very difficult conditions. Saturday and Sunday nights were the worst, she claimed. "There were nothing but rows and the amount of destruction was very bad." Mrs. Phelan concluded by saying a lot of people were frightened and the Gardai were beseeched

ATTEMPT TO BURN FINE GAEL CARAVAN

Gardai are investigating an attempt to burn the Fine Gael caravan which is sited in The Parade, Kilkenny, on Tuesday night. A back window was broken and a fire started inside. Gardai are awaiting the results of forensic evidence before they say how the fire started. Carmel Boyd, P.R.O., Kilkenny District Executive, Fine Gael, said the attempt was a deliberate act by supporters of another political party. It was noticeable, she said, that two nearby caravans belonging to other parties were not touched.

Garret FitzGerald in Waterford with party candidates, Katharine Bulbulia, Eddie Collins and Austin Deasy.

INFLATION RATE "CAUSING TERRIBLE DAMAGE"

— COLLINS

During a recent Dail debate on the Employers' employment contribution scheme bill, 1981, Deputy Eddie Collins, referred to what he described as the "very difficult circumstances" under which Irish Leathers Ltd., had been

O'Beirne, stated that the County Engineer "should cop himself on." The Commissioners had requested the provision of a wire mesh fence around the town dump in an effort to prevent rubbish being washed away by the tide and on

---

of Fianna Fáil was second with 8,314. Eddie Collins, Fine Gael, and Billy Kenneally, Fianna Fáil, also took seats. The other candidates secured first preference votes as follows: Billy Kyne of Labour got 1,532 votes; Paddy Gallagher 3,453; Brian Swift, Fianna Fáil, 3,456 and Katherine Bulbulia, Fine Gael, (a large gatherer of the growing women's vote) 3,691.

A Northern Ireland H-Block hunger striker, Kevin Lynch had been selected to stand in Waterford and got a surprising 3,333 votes, upsetting the Labour vote and that of SFWP.

Munster Express *man wins seat*
In 1982 Paddy Gallagher of SFWP, a *Munster Express* staffer, won a Dáil seat. J. J. Walsh organised a special celebration in the *Munster Express*, a day after the count. Following party policy, Gallagher went on to become a full time TD. Gallagher was one of three SFWP candidates elected to the Dáil. Together with Tony Gregory, Independent TD from Dublin Central, these deputies held the balance of power.

After concessions they voted for Charles Haughey as Taoiseach, with independent John O'Connell as Ceann Comhairle. There was drama on the day of the formation of the government, when SFWP delegates nearly missed the vote as the Dáil bell was called and only managed to get into the Dáil by jumping down from the Press Gallery, which was the only door open at the time. Rebuilding works in the Dáil mean that this option is no longer available.

As a result of a series of grotesque mishaps, the government did not last long, and led to an autumn election in 1982, which a combination of Fine Gael and Labour won. Paddy Gallagher unfortunately lost his seat which Independent Tom Brennan took, and Fianna Fáil won back a seat.

There was much anger at the count. Clover workers picketed all candidates during the election in a campaign to get their claim. For the first time the two party leaders argued in front of RTÉ cameras, but the great television debate on the election was called a bore by the Editor, J. J. Walsh.

Cattle die en route to Egypt

Animal lovers were shocked when 70 cattle being exported live died on a ship leaving Waterford port en route to Egypt. The boat was a converted banana boat from Wales on which live cattle were herded before being slaughtered on board. More stringent regulations on the transport of cattle would follow.

FAI cup win

In 1983 the Waterford soccer team eventually won the FAI cup after victory over St Patricks' Athletic in Dalymount Park with a scoreline of 1–0. The winning goal was scored by Brian Gardiner, a native of Preston in England, he had played with famous Preston North End. Tommy Jackson, ex Manchester United, Everton and Nottingham Forest was the player manager to achieve this goal that had eluded Waterford all through the glorious 1960s and 1970s, when the Waterford team won five League titles in seven

seasons. There were great celebrations when the cup was eventually brought over the Redmond Bridge.

Olympic medal for Treacy

The great sporting triumph of 1984 was John Treacy's Olympic medal in Los Angeles. The marathon runner was born in 1957 in Villierstown near Dungarvan and won silver with a strong race, starting down the field but working his way steadily up until he entered the stadium in third place. He clinched his medal by overtaking British athlete Charles Spedding with 150 metres to go. As usual *Munster Express* Editor J. J. Walsh was there to see Ireland's Olympic success.

New courthouse

In 1984 Waterford would finally get a fine new courthouse, with the Office of Public Works doing a major refurbishment

Austin Deasy

Dungarvan man Austin Deasy became a senior Cabinet Minister after the Fine Gael/Labour success. He was to hold this position until the general election in 1987. As Minister for Agriculture Austin Deasy became a great negotiator for the Irish farmer interest in Brussels, which stopped Ireland going into major recession in the 1980s. He also managed to secure a major re-vamp of Ardkeen Hospital and get it upgraded to Regional Hospital status. This was despite much local county opposition, where local county hospital treatments would be cut back and centralised at Waterford Regional Hospital.

At this time there were increasing and controversial health cuts and Minister for Health Barry Desmond was subject to harsh criticism. Local health board meetings were the scene of fierce debate and featured strongly in the *Munster Express*.

JET SHERIDAN OIL DISTRIBUTORS WATERFORD
Tractor Diesel: | Motor Diesel | Heating Oils
It will pay you to contact us! 'Phone: 051/72891

The Munster Express

LAST EDITION **32 PAGES**

Incorporating "The Waterford Citizen," "The Celt," and "The Waterford Standard." — EXPRESS DELIVERY BRITAIN 30p

Registered at the General Post Office as a Newspaper | 122nd YEAR | Friday, 12th June, 1981 | PRICE: 25p including Value Added Tax.

A cheerful group of party workers pictured at the Military Barracks Polling Booth yesterday - while on right, Alderman Paddy Gallagher, Sinn Fein the Workers' Party Candidate was the first to arrive for the count at the Courthouse this morning where he was greeted by Court Officer, Seamus O'Neill; Paddy was accompanied by Brian Sheehan, journalist and S.F.W.P. Director of Finance, Billy McCarthy.

(Eoin Murphy)

SWING TO FINE GAEL

As votes were being sorted in the General Election this Friday morning, a positive swing to Fine Gael was emerging in Waterford and Kilkenny. Around the country there was about a 7% swing to Fine Gael in some areas while in others the Government was holding its own. At this stage the final outcome of the election as a whole looks like it will be a very close fight with marginal seats playing a vital role in the closing stages.

In Waterford, tallymen figures, which are usually reliable, indicated that at about halfway through the sorting, Fine Gael were ahead with 46% of first preferences compared to 37% for Fianna Fail. Labour took about 4%, while S.W.F.P. received 7%. The H-Block candidate was polling very well with 6%.

Individually Austin Deasy, F.G., looks a sure bet to head the poll with an estimated 6,000 of Fine Gael's combined 12,182. Jackie Fahey looks like being the second home with a large share of Fianna Fail's total going to him. No breakdown of the Fianna Fail fugures were available but William Kenneally seems to be second to Jackie Fahey with Brian Swift also doing well. Eddie Collins is polling extremely well although he has Katherine Bulbulia close on his heels.

When Austin Deasy is elected it will be very interesting to see where his surplus goes. At the moment Eddie Collins looks like taking the third seat with William Kenneally taking the fourth. S.F.W.P. did not do as well as

AUSTIN DEASY to top the poll.

JACKIE FAHEY expected runner-up to Austin Deasy.

EDDIE COLLINS likely to take third seat.

WILLIE KENNEALLY also expected to be elected.

This election's poll is estimated to be 79% compared to 78% at the last General Election.

The wet weather was responsible for one of the slowest starts to an election for years but as the day progressed the people came out in strength and some booths recorded the highest poll for decades. Dungarvan, in particular, had one of its most intensive voting days ever with the nine booths at three centres providing an average poll of 81%. The four booths in the Waterford Regional College returned a massive 88% poll.

The turnout in South Tipperary is estimated to have

WATERFORD GLASS ON BUDGET FOR 1981

Waterford Glass is doing "extremely well" so far this year following a disappointing performance in 1980 which saw pre-tax profits fall by 31% to £8m. on a turnover of £154m. So stated the company's secretary, Mr. Owen Kealy after its annual general meeting on Tuesday.

According to Mr. Kealy the dollar's surge is giving the company a useful boost with markets "buoyant" for its crystal in the U.S. and Canada. Despite increasing its prices there by 12%, at the beginning of 1981, the strength of the dollar and heavy demand have enabled it to improve its sales in the two lucrative American markets.

The home market is also holding up better in the current year, Mr. Kealy pointed out. "Things are looking very well compared to last year. We're right on budget for 1981."

The current year has seen a "recovery" at the Switzer Group, which had what Mr. Kealy described as a "disastrous" year in 1980. In addition, he said, that the company were hoping that the present strike at Switzers, which is confined to a very small number of employees, would "fizzle out" shortly.

Mr. Kealy revealed that the current year is going well for the Smith Group, which distributes Renault cars. He explained that the Smith Group had managed to increase its sales against expectations and added "What we've lost on the swings we've gained on the roundabouts."

Earlier at the meeting, and in reply to a shareholder's query, Mr. Kealy had stated that the company's debt to equity ratio was "quite low". He explained that there had been no revelation of the company's assets since 1975, but that this would take place this year and would tie in with the company's assets since 1975, but that this would take place this year and would tie in with the company's publication of its current cost accounts. With regard to the company's share capital, he said: "The board of directors feels that there is no necessity at the moment for a rights issue."

In reply to a shareholder's question on the industrial relations within the company Waterford's Mr. Colm O'Connell replied that following a

meeting with workers' representatives earlier this year, the company was receiving 100%, co-operation from its employees. The company's chairman, Mr. Patrick McGrath, said: "Relations with the employees are, as far as I'm concerned, satisfactory."

Personality Portrait

55 WORKERS TO BE LAID OFF AT SMURFIT PLASTICS

As part of the settlement of the Smurfit Plastics 11 week old strike at Grannagh, more than half the workforce are being laid off.

Under the terms of a rationalisation agreement, 55 workers will lose their jobs, bringing the number employed at the plant down to 39.

The company is to cease production of plyurethane film sheeting for the agricultural industry but will continue with the making of plastic sacks.

Ten of the workers to be made redundant have rejected offers of compensation which were accepted by the majority of the employees. The factory will remain closed until agreement is reached with them.

Waterford Crystal expands and contracts

The mid 1980s would see Waterford Crystal expand its profits under the strong dollar. A progressive profit-sharing scheme enabled workers to benefit from the success. However, the McGrath family, who were long-term strategic shareholders, sold over half of their holding at this time to the London-based investment group Globe Investments.

The new owners brought in the well known Paddy Hayes from the Ford Ireland group, causing some concern that he might 'rationalise' the Glass as he did at Ford.

In 1986 Waterford Glass expanded by buying the famous Wedgwood Group in England. They already owned Aynsley China and knew the market. The share price climbed but eventually cost savings would be needed. Waterford was now the largest tableware company in the world.

Under Paddy Hayes, the company's ambitions soared. Redmond O'Donoghue of Ford Spain was brought back to his native Waterford for marketing the expanded Group.

By the autumn of 1987 however, for the first time a major redundancy announcement was made in what was the end of an era at 'the Glass'. Two factors were blamed for this. Firstly, the US dollar, the currency of the major market, was falling in value. Secondly, bank debt was high and costs were too high.

Despite the union, who did not want voluntary redundancies and opposed compulsory ones, almost 1,000 workers would take the package. Waterford Glass remained the large largest local employers with over 2,350 employees across their factories in Dungarvan, Butlerstown (where they made lighting ware) and the main factory in Kilbarry.

In 1986 Taoiseach Garret Fitzgerald opened the Waterford Crystal Gallery in Kilbarry, a brainchild of Redmond O'Donoghue, a future chief executive.

The liberal agenda

Throughout the 1980s there was a national tussle between traditional Catholic moral views and the proponents of more liberal attitudes. The place of abortion, divorce and contraception in Irish society was debated with passion and intensity. Waterford generally supported the more conservative view.

In the abortion referendum of 1983, which attempted to copperfasten the ban in the Constitution, Waterford voted 2–1 in favour. The Church was vocal on this issue and on divorce, where a referendum proposing to make it available to Irish citizens was defeated in 1986. Mass attendance was still strong in this period but waned within a decade and a half as Church scandals broke. In the second divorce referendum ten years later Waterford still voted 'no', but with a greatly reduced majority.

The *Munster Express* did not follow the Church's conservative view but opted for social reform. The voters, however, held still to the conservative viewpoint.

John Walsh and Declan Waters, anti-divorce campaigners

Poster advertising during the abortion referendum in 1983

Local broadcasting

In 1987 the debate on the legalising of local radio threatened the *Munster Express*' position. The Fine Gael/Labour coalition could not agree, and RTÉ unions wanted local public sector broadcasting. The incoming Fianna Fáil minority Government wanted a private sector solution but would limit newspaper involvement to 35 per cent.

The *Munster Express* would put in a proposal with Waterford Foods, a major food PLC, and RTÉ broadcaster, Pat Butler, and local businesses Darrer Stores and Walsh's Car Sales but failed in its licence quest. Ray Burke was the Communications Minister at the time, and apparently resisted the idea of newspapers being involved in local broadcasting. The *Limerick Leader* failed in a similar bid though the *Claire Champion* and the *Connacht Tribune* were more successful.

In the end the existing pirate station WLR was a popular choice locally, with a number of local shareholders investing in the new company. They eventually made it into a success and sold their shares to the Cork-based newspaper group, Thomas Crosbie Holdings, with founder Des Whelan holding onto his stake.

PDs win seat with Cullen

The 1987 election saw a shift to the right in Irish politics. Progressive Democrat TD Martin Cullen was the local standard bearer. He later become a Cabinet minister and by relentless lobbying on behalf of Waterford from that position was able to deliver a motorway to Waterford and many more investments. In that election the PDs took one of the Fine Gael seats and Labour took a Fianna Fáil seat. Fine Gael realised that it would take decades to win this Cullen vote back, although they did very well in council elections. Waterford would thus become a marginal constituency and begin to get more attention.

In the 1989 election Cullen lost his seat, but was appointed to the Senate. Austin Deasy had lost his Cabinet seat in 1987, so now Waterford had no representation at the Cabinet. The job losses at Waterford Glass would see the city lobby for more funding from Government and try to emulate the success of Galway and Limerick with their universities and Cabinet ministers. Waterford now wanted attention and investment at a time when Galway had outpaced Waterford in population, industry and influence. The University campaign would see Waterford strive to play catch-up with the other provincial cities such as Limerick which had been awarded a university even with Galway so close.

Enhancements to the College and Institute would follow but the goal of University would not be reached, despite industry and business groups demanding it for the south east and giving equality for the region as industry migrated to the university cities looking for high tech students and workers. The campaigning *Munster Express* pushed hard for renewed ministerial representation for Waterford.

Eventually, Martin Cullen, who had become disillusioned with the PD leadership, joined Fianna Fáil. Local lobby groups saw him as a rising star. He topped the poll in the 1997 election and was appointed Minister of State and in 2002 Minister for the Environment. Cullen would ensure that motorways would be delivered and the Waterford Regional Technical College upgraded to Institute of Technology status, but rivalries would ensure that other RTCs would get similar treatment.

H-Block hunger striker stands for election in Waterford

In 1981 a Northern Ireland H-Block hunger striker, Kevin Lynch, was selected to stand in Waterford and got a surprising 3,333 votes, upsetting the Labour vote and that of SFWP, where local candidate, Alderman Paddy Gallagher, was tipped to win a seat. Many factory workers voted for the H-Block candidate.

A number of demonstrations were held in the months running up to the election supporting the strikers' five demands, with workers taking time off work to demonstrate. Election workers recall some level of intimidation at the time and a tense election. Lynch was the seventh hunger striker to die, in August 1981.

John Treacy, Olympic medallist 1984

The third Waterford athlete to compete at the Olympics was John Treacy from Villierstown. In his first ever Olympic marathon he took the silver medal in Los Angeles in 1984. Treacy also competed in three other Olympics. His first was in Moscow in 1980 when he collapsed unconscious on the track in the heats of the 10,000 metres on a very humid day. A few days later he ran in the heats of the 5,000 metres and easily made the final to finish 7th, three places behind Eamon Coghlan. He also competed in the 1988 and 1992 Olympics.

Treacy was known as a tenacious runner who did not have a particularly sharp final kick in the track races. He did occasionally suffer also from bad luck, however. In the 1978 European Athletics Championships in Prague, then Czechoslovakia, he was placed 11th in the fast 10,000 metres race and fourth in the slow and tactical 5,000 metres race, losing to the winner, Italy's Venanzio Ortis, by just 3/10ths of a second. In the 5,000 metres final, he may have lost the chance of a medal by lingering behind Great Britain's Nick Rose on the final back straight, just after Rose had dropped from the lead group.

John Treacy was a brilliant cross country athlete. After finishing third in the World Junior Championships twice, he had a fantastic win in Glasgow in 1978 in the Senior race and then one year later in front of 30,000 fans on Limerick Racecourse he retained the title. This has been described as one of the greatest performances of all time by an Irish sportsperson on Irish soil.

He won the British AAA Junior 3,000 metres twice and 5,000 metres and Senior 10,000 metres titles as well. He won five All Ireland 5,000 metres and the 10,000 metres twice and seven individual inter county cross country titles. Before this he had an outstanding career on the American collegiate circuit with Providence College. He was the first sportsman to be awarded the Freedom of Waterford. His brother Ray was also a national champion and his twin sister Liz was also a fine athlete. John's career lasted almost twenty-five years.

After the Los Angeles Olympics, Treacy still ran competitively until 1995, retiring following a road race held in his honour in Waterford, attended by the other two medallists from the 1984 Olympic marathon, Carlos Lopes and Charlie Spedding. While he did not win any more major international championships medals, Treacy won the 1992 Los Angeles marathon. In the 1986 European Athletics Championships in Stuttgart, then West Germany,

John Treacy

he placed sixth in the 10,000 metres race. In the 1987 World Athletics Championships in Rome, he placed 26th in the 10,000 metres race and 13th in the 5,000 metres final.

John Treacy is currently chief executive of the Irish Sports Council. He is married to Fionnuala and they have four children, Caoimhe and Deirdre, Seán and Conor.

Waterford athletics

Patricia Walsh

In 1984 Patricia Walsh, a native of Ferrybank, reached the discus final at the Olympics and finished a very creditable ninth—one place higher would have got her into the final three throws. Patricia was a senior international at the age of sixteen and won the FISEC Games discus title as a juvenile. She twice came second in the British senior discus and won the Irish discus title on nine occasions, the shot putt twice and javelin once and competed at the European Junior and Senior Championships. She still holds the Irish discus record set back in 1984. In 1981 she went to the University of Tennessee on an athletics scholarship and won at the famous Penn relays meeting and was five times an All American champion.

Brendan and Shane Quinn

Next on the list of Waterford Olympians was Brendan Quinn, another product of De La Salle. He went to Providence on a scholarship and had a very successful time there; here in Ireland he was 3,000 metres steeplechase champion on three occasions—1982, 1985 and 1988, and he still holds the Irish record for the event. He also won an inter county cross country individual title. He was selected to compete in three Olympics but was ruled out through injury in two. In the European championships in

1986 he had the misfortune to fall in his heat and again he had to withdraw through injury. Eventually, he competed in 1988 in the 3,000 metres steeplechase and reached the semi final.

Brendan Quinn's 18-year-old son Shane is one of the finest middle distance runners in Ireland with a host of under age national titles; he won a silver medal for the 3000 metres at the 2010 European Youth Olympics Festival.

Susan Smith

Susan Smith, who started her career as a juvenile with St Paul's and then became a senior with Waterford AC, competed at two Olympics. After losing a few years due to a major injury she battled back to fitness and in 1996 she reached the semi final of the 400 metres hurdles. She finished fifth, missing out by just one place to make the final despite setting a new Irish record. In 1997 she had excellent results at Grand Prix meetings and at the World Championships. She reached the final of the 400 metres hurdles where she finished seventh but again set a new Irish record at the meeting.

At the European Championships in 1998, after finishing first in her semi final she finished eighth in the final. In her second Olympics in 2000 she did not proceed beyond round one. Susan was one of the greatest ever juvenile athletes in Ireland and she went on to be a super competitive senior athlete and won eight All Ireland Senior 100 metres hurdles and five 400 metres hurdles titles between 1989 and 2000. She held numerous Irish records and also won a British AAA title.

Jamie Costin

Waterford's current Olympian is race walker Jamie Costin of West Waterford AC who competes in the gruelling 50 kilometres event. Costin has competed at two Olympic

Games and was chosen for a third, but a horrific car crash a few days before the Games in Athens in 2004 left him with many broken bones in his back and it looked as if his athletic career was over. Remarkably, he fought his way back to full health and returned to pounding the roads. He made the World Championships in 2007 but retired during the race. In his first Olympics in 2000 he finished 38th and in the 2001 World Championships he finished 28th. In the 2003 World Championships he was disqualified and in the Beijing Olympics of 2008 he finished 44th. He has won All Ireland titles over 10,000 metres, 35 kilometres and 50 kilometres and holds the Irish record in the 50 kilometres.

Athletic tradition maintained
In the present time the proud Waterford tradition in athletics is being carried on admirably by a number of young athletes. This year David McCarthy from Ballinamult, a member of West Waterford AC, finished third in the European under-23 5,000 metres championship and became Waterford's first ever sub four minute miler.

Kelly Proper of Ferrybank was 6th in the final of the long jump at the same championships and recently won the All Ireland long jump title for the fourth successive year and the 200 metres for the second year in succession; she also holds an all round title and is the Irish long jump record holder.

Kate Veale from West Waterford is a star under-age walker with British under-age titles to her credit in record times. Niamh Whelan is a star junior sprinter.

Red Kettle Theatre Company
by LIAM MURPHY

Now in its 25th year, Red Kettle Theatre has survived as a professional theatre company, despite savage funding reductions and several changes in direction.

There was a sense of economic and physical expansion back in the 1970s and Waterford city grew out into local authority housing estates like St John's Park. As a result of improved education, better libraries and radio and television, young people sought outlets for creative interests and needed arts and arts centres.

This initially manifested itself in a very loose co-operative of like minds and similar dreams. The Waterford Arts for All project emerged with that objective and campaigned for broader arts availability and for an arts centre.

Egalitarian and mildly socialist principles informed the participants who formed an Arts For All Theatre Company which brought plays to pubs and public venues as well as bringing a children's play to housing estates and anywhere there was a residents' committee.

The group featured Jim Nolan and Ben and Tony Hennessy and they conceived a desire to expand out and create a professional theatre company, the first one in Waterford. Jim Nolan was starting to write plays and it seemed a natural progression to form a company; it was to be called Red Kettle. Jim Nolan was ambitious, talented and filled with words and dreams. In those early days he shared that with people working in local radio such as Clodagh Walsh, and with Eoin Ronayne, the Hennesseys and the wonderful Meagher family, also from St John's Park.

Tom Hickey, (Benjy of 'The Riordans'), Jim Nolan (playwright) and John Thompson (amateur actor and undertaker) preparing for the Red Kettle production of Nolan's play 'Moonshine'.

Jim Nolan's first plays for Red Kettle were performed in the Garter Lane Arts Centre and with the late Tony Ryan on board it was decided to hire the Theatre Royal for Jim's play about the jute factory workers, *The Gods Are Angry Miss Kerr*. Current Waterford Mayor Mary Roche was among the early players.

In those early years production values were important and using as many local actors and technicians as possible Red Kettle shone brightly and importantly. Ben Hennessy and Liam Meagher began to write and direct for Little Red Kettle and forged a change in the national view of the involvement and importance of theatre in education.

Alongside this, Jim Nolan as Artistic Director was championing new writing and in those years his own plays, *The Guernica Hotel*, *Moonshine* and the amazing *The Salvage Shop* were confirming not just Jim Nolan's place in Irish theatre, but copperfastening Red Kettle as a major theatre company. Nolan went on to national and international notice, while continuing to live in Waterford.

Red Kettle continued down a new road under Ben Hennessy's stewardship. It was a difficult task without Jim Nolan, T.V. Honan and Liam Rellis. The arts climate had changed, ambitions had to be sharper, funding was tighter and a very administratively-minded Arts Council had to wield a knife deeply into dreams.

Ben Hennessy took the company down the spectacle route with big adventurous productions in a circus tent. The timing in winter of *Riddley Walker* was unfortunate but the very popular prices for *A Midsummer's Night Dream* won back a hesitant public. Red Kettle are now actively pursuing with City Council the possibility of purchasing a circus tent to increase the spectacle and do wonderful creative things. The survival of Red Kettle is a tribute to its tenacity and desire to provide first-class quality productions and is a testament to the hardy band of optimists who burned with a shared zeal and ambition.

Seán Kelly, Waterford's great cyclist

John James 'Seán' Kelly, the world class cyclist, was raised in Carrigduff, near Clonea Power. He was actually born in the Belleville Nursing Home, so Waterford rightfully claims him, but Carrick on Suir is where he learned his cycling. He is a hero in both locations and has also received the Freedom of Waterford honour for his international cycling successes.

In Carrick's colours, he became national junior champion. Missing the 1976 Montreal Olympics, he decided to go to Europe and there became a professional in 1977. He won numerous road racing titles in France, Italy, Spain and Belgium, and won the Green jersey on the Tour de France four times. He won the Paris–Nice race seven times, the Paris–Roubaix race in 1984 and 1986, and the Tour of Spain in 1988.

At home, Waterford people followed his career with pride. During the Freedom of the City presentation a local politician recalled how we used to ask during the Tour de France, 'how was Kelly doing?', since in those days before the internet the best news we could get were sketchy radio reports.

Back home he won the Tour of Ireland Nissan Classics four times, beating many international challengers. The Tour passed through Waterford and Carrick on Suir and the Quays were packed to cheer on their local hero.

He and fellow-Irishman Paul McQuaid were critical in persuading the Tour de France organisers to provide an Irish start for the 1998 Tour to mark the 1798 rebellion. Through him and Michael Hearn the *Munster Express* ran many exclusives on the Tour de France and to mark its coming to Ireland, the *Munster Express* followed the style of French newspapers and did a special colour supplement on the Tour de France. The Irish stage passed through

Waterford, Dungarvan and Carrick on Suir on its way to Cork from Enniscorthy, the centre of the 1798 anniversary, having started in Dublin the day before.

Seán Kelly now works for Eurosport as a commentator, living back with his family near Carrick on Suir. He also raises money for charity through the Blazing Saddles cycle event for the National Council for the Blind.

A book on Seán Kelly, *The Man for All Seasons*, written by Slieverue man and sports writer with the *Sunday Times*, David Walsh, who went to school in Waterpark, sold well, perhaps because Kelly gave so few interviews to the media. Kelly was popular with his team mates, but was known to the sporting press as taciturn, self-reliant, physically strong, focused, enduring and with a hard courage that they often attributed to his farming background.

A fluent French speaker, Kelly was very popular in France and that meant that the world famous Tour de France with cyclists like Marco Pantani would come to Ireland. The Sports Centre in Carrick is named after him as is an academy in Belgium.

Dawn Run

The racehorse Dawn Run, with strong Waterford connections, was the most successful race mare in the history of National Hunt racing. She won the Champion Hurdle at the Cheltenham racing festival in 1984 and the Cheltenham Gold Cup over fences at the festival in 1986. Dawn Run was the only racehorse ever to have completed the Champion Hurdle-Gold Cup double. She was one of only two mares who have managed to win the Champion Hurdle, and of only four who have won the Cheltenham Gold Cup. She was also the only horse ever to complete the English, Irish and French Champion Hurdle treble.

A daughter of the highly successful National Hunt sire Deep Run, Dawn Run was bought for 5,800 guineas and trained by Paddy Mullins in Ireland. She started her career at the age of four, running in flat races at provincial courses. Remarkably, she was ridden in her first three races by her 62-year-old owner Charmian Hill. After winning on her third and fourth starts she set out on her hurdling career and progressed through the ranks to become champion novice hurdler in Britain and Ireland in her first season, 1982–3.

In her second season she won eight of her nine races including the English Champion Hurdle at Cheltenham, the Irish Champion Hurdle at Leopardstown, both over two miles, and the French Champion Hurdle (Grande Course de Haies d'Auteuil) at Auteuil over three miles, becoming the first horse ever to complete the treble. Her other big victories that season included the Christmas Hurdle (2 miles) at Kempton, in which she beat the reigning champion hurdler Gay Brief by a neck after a thrilling duel up the home stretch, the Sandemans Hurdle at Aintree (2.5 miles), which she won in a canter by 15 lengths, and the Prix La Barka in Auteuil.

She turned to steeple chasing the following season but was injured after winning her first race and was out of action for the rest of the season. The decision was then made by her owner to send her back to France to try and repeat her 1984 win in the French Champion Hurdle. Sadly, in that race she fell at a hurdle on the back straight and never got up again. It subsequently transpired that she had suffered a fatal heart attack. It was a measure of the great affection that was felt for her that her death was reported on the front page of the following day's *Irish Times*, and her statue now adorns the parade ring at Cheltenham, opposite the statue of Arkle.

Munster Express in the 1970s and 1980s

Inflation was a big problem in the 1970s, affecting all Irish industry. Newsprint rose substantially in price in the 1970s after the oil crisis of 1973. This was also a period of high inflation, high interest rates and bank strikes which hit cash flow.

National wage agreements were also a major cost for business and in the 1980s the costs proved too high as the economy began to falter. This proved to be a very challenging time and some newspapers did not last the pace, both nationally and locally. In the southeast the *Waterford Post* collapsed, as did the *Kilkenny Standard*, and *Echo* in Enniscorthy, though the latter was to come back under the Buttle ownership. Bucking the trend, *Munster Express* staff numbers expanded in the 1970s and moved into new premises nearby, to what had had been a garage known as Scanlons, which had a local dealership for UK cars such as Austin Rover.

The press room was extended. A Kilkenny edition had been launched in 1968, but this was later dropped in the advertising recession of the early 1980s. Some staff moved on in the early 1980s, including the famous Paddy

Editor J. J. Walsh and his daughter Priscilla in the pressroom

Gallagher, who became a TD and under SFWP party rules had to resign his position. Unfortunately, his tenure as a TD did not last as long as expected and he later returned to the newspaper business, first with a paper for the unemployed and then a free newspaper that is still produced today.

J. J.'s son Nicholas joined the paper in 1971/2 having studied production management in the London College of Printing. As well as being involved in the installation of web offset printing in 1974/5 he also contributed to news editing and editorial development. Priscilla Walsh (one of J. J. Walsh's daughters) had come into the business after studying at journalism college in Rathmines College and Trinity College in Dublin, where she did languages. She assisted her father in the editing and writing duties. Her brother Kieran, who had worked as a financial journalist in Dublin, joined the paper in 1984 and became advertising manager in 1984. He also wrote articles and stood in for news editor Priscilla in holiday periods. She moved to London at the end of that decade, and Kieran acted as both advertising manager and news editor until John O'Connor became news editor.

The advertising market eventually did improve. Davy Daniels was main advertising representative and he was assisted by various advertising reps. As the economy burgeoned in the late 1980s the advertising market improved and demand rose. In 1989 two more colour printing units were added to the press, enabling an extra four pages to be published every week, and making front page editorial and advertising possible. In 2005 a new press gave 80 per cent colour. Colour did not necessarily add to circulation but did give a traditional newspaper a more modern look.

The extra building work required to house the new press meant that the machine took a little longer than planned to get up and running. By this time over 80 per cent of the newspaper is in colour. With the boom in property advertising good times seemed assured, but as with all economic cycles, the boom ended. The *Munster Express*, however, had made its investment in good time and could now weather the crisis even if print runs had to be trimmed.

The wheelchair incident

In September 1986 the *Munster Express* editor made front page national news headlines. Taoiseach Garret FitzGerald had been invited by Waterford Crystal to open their new crystal gallery in Waterford. This all went along efficiently, but afterwards the minders refused to hold a press conference as the Taoiseach did not want to meet *Munster Express* Editor, J. J. Walsh. A six-month-old editorial called 'Divorce Dilemma' was the reason proffered.

In a typically rambling article, ostensibly about the forthcoming divorce referendum, the 80-year-old Editor declared that the Taoiseach should not 'encumber' himself by propelling his incapacitated wife in a wheelchair 'in full view of everybody and significantly the television cameras'. He went on to describe how in the United States 'most well-circumstanced men' deliberately severed the marital links, discarding menopausal first wives for younger models. At this time the old method of evolving the editorials with an experienced staff member had been abandoned, and this was a pity.

A provincial newspaper like the *Munster Express* would usually not be a priority read for a Dublin-based prime minister, but it seems he did take offence at this rather outspoken piece.

When questioned by David Hanly on RTÉ's *Morning Ireland*, J. J. Walsh, woken up early out of bed, was a little tetchy and said that when he played golf he got a caddy—this was not tactful.

Disabled groups got angry at the tone of the piece, and there were many complaints to J. J.'s house and office. J. J. went off to Spain to let the fuss die down, leaving his son Kieran (then advertising manager, now Editor) to look after the office and apologise to those who took offence.

As was his way, however, J. J. remained unrepentant. He explained that he had not wished to offend the Taoiseach but wanted something done about the country at a time of mass unemployment and business closure. In fact he felt victimised and later on RTÉ's *Nationwide* he explained his theory that the press conference had really

been cancelled because of the Taoiseach's wish to avoid the Collins controversy: Minister of State Eddie Collins had attended a private company meeting of Clover Meats but had not disclosed it. Two weeks later Collins was sacked from his office at the Department of Trade, having refused the Taoiseach's request that he should resign. J. J. saw the *Munster Express* editorial being used as an excuse to avoid controversy in Waterford at a time when there was a huge financial crisis in the country. He got support in Waterford, where his regular readers, used to his style, saw an elderly editor getting a hard time.

After this incident the newspaper became one of the best-known provincial newspapers in Ireland. The role of a smaller newspaper could be seen to be important after all and there was some sneaking admiration for J. J. Walsh and his ability to get publicity. Advertising agencies had now all heard of the *Munster Express*, and when Kieran as advertising manager went around seeking business, the paper was always number one on the schedule.

Taoiseach Garret FitzGerald and his wife Joan

Eddie and Leila Collins

The 1990s

The decade of the 1990s

Internationally, the big story of 1990 was the Gulf War as Saddam Hussein of Iraq invaded Kuwait, threatening dominate world oil supplies. George Bush senior mobilised an international force to invade Kuwait in turn to expel Saddam.

On a lighter note, summer 1990 was the Irish soccer team's first great success in the World Cup. Jack Charlton's team progressed to the quarter-finals by a triumphant series of draws before being beaten by the host country, Italy.

In Waterford, the big story of 1990 was concern over the situation for Waterford Crystal, as Waterford Glass had recently been renamed, being now one division of the Waterford Wedgwood Group.

Managing Director Dr Paddy Galvin warned workers that they had to accept change or face serious consequences. A few months later a strike was called after holiday bonus payments were withheld as part of a cost

Noah's Ark being hoisted on to the Quay during a Spraoí festiva;

cutting process. As crises do, the 14-week strike increased interest in the *Munster Express* as people anxiously followed its progress. The loss of earnings caused the retail trade in Waterford to suffer. Eventually, Bertie Ahern, then Minister for Labour, intervened, and a compromise was reached.

Paddy Galvin, a former managing director of Guinness, where he had carried out a major rationalisation, produced a plan to save the business. In 1990 and 1991 the combined losses were £6m on sales of £150m; the value of the key US market dropped by one-third in 1991. New investors Tony O'Reilly and Morgan Stanley, who had purchased a substantial stake in the company, saw the value of their investment drop significantly.

Nearly 2,000 Waterford Crystal workers met in the Ardree Hotel where unions told workers of the elements of the plan, which included halving the number of lines produced, development of a visitor centre in Waterford, redundancies, short time working, reduced holiday pay and later retirement age. One third of the staff were to lose their jobs over four years, wages and salaries were cut by 25 per cent, and a four-year pay freeze was imposed.

Tramore Racecourse for sale again
In the same January 1991, the worry about the future of Tramore racing dissipated as the Fleming family announced that there would be no property sale as tenders received for the racecourse did not meet their expectations. Two decades later the racecourse is for sale again, as the directors seek to move to a new location near the Back Strand.

Seán Kelly christens his children
In March 1991 the famous cyclist Seán Kelly and his wife Linda brought their recently born twins Nigel and Stacey to St Molleran's Church in Carrick-on-Suir to be christened.

Bausch and Lomb expand
Bausch and Lomb announced a major expansion in the 600-strong workforce with 440 more workers to be added in four years.

Veteran editor dies
September 1992 marked the passing of the *Munster Express'* veteran editor and owner J. J. Walsh. The reaction to his death is covered elsewhere, but this obviously meant major changes to the paper, as his son Kieran took over the reins. Initially he was both advertising and news editor, later John O'Connor, well known for his broadcasting in RTÉ, became news editor and started to put a new shape to the newspaper.

Dr William Lee, Bishop of Waterford, chats with Taoiseach Albert Reynolds at the opening of Bellvue port

Mayor of Waterford

Martin Cullen became Mayor of Waterford in 1993. He was the PD party spokesman on Enterprise and Employment. He fell out with party leader Mary Harney over nominations for the European elections and left the party in 1994. He was pursuaded by Albert Reynolds to join Fianna Fáil. He was a member of the Fianna Fáil/PD coalition from 1992, serving as Minister for Transport in which role he had a major influence on the motorway to Waterford. During his tenure the newly formed National Roads Authority opened an office in Tramore.

Paddy Galvin retires

In 1996 Dr Paddy Galvin retired from Waterford Crystal, having seen the company through tumultuous times but getting the firm back to profit. This was unfortunately not to last, and thirteen years after his retirement the firm closed.

Christmas storm

The *Munster Express* had dramatic pictures of the great Christmas Eve storm of 1997, regarded as the worst in living memory. Trees and power lines were down all over the county.

Tour d'Irlande

The great event of 1998 was the holding of a stage of the Tour de France in Ireland. Master-minded by Seán Kelly and earlier by Stephen Roche, there was great debate about where the overnight stage between the start in Dublin and the finish in Cork should be. In the event it was given to Enniscorthy to mark the 200th anniversary of the Rising of 1798.

On the way, the famous cycle race passed the *Munster Express* offices on the Quay. Staff of the paper had a wine and cheese party to celebrate.

A spectacular Ferrybank crash: the lorry (above) was driven by an Italian driver, whose brakes failed coming down a steep hill on Rockshire Road, Ferrybank. The driver was later commended by gardaí for his bravery and skill in keeping the lorry in some control prior to crashing. But for him there could have been injuries or loss of life. Astonished residents at the scene (below), contemplate property damage, but nothing worse.

Dockside scenes in the 1990s

The newspaper in the 1990s

The year 1991 initiated major administrative changes on the newspaper; management consultants were brought in to assist and plan for the future. More flexibility with staff replaced what had been sometimes a hard line in the past and new technology agreements were brought in. In the less authoritarian atmosphere, staff parties became big events.

There was a generally positive atmosphere as the city of Waterford began to improve as the decade progressed. Jobs and property advertising expanded, as did motors as the demand for new cars replaced the previous adequate second hand cars market. National advertisers adopted colour and the move to colour continued in the *Munster Express* with more print units added from the UK in 1996 and again at the end of the decade with the purchase of the *Leinster Leader* press.

The Internet

Kieran Walsh identified the internet as a new opportunity for newspapers, boosting overseas readership. The *Munster Express* became the first Irish regional newspaper to follow *The Irish Times* on to the web.

Danny Meadows of the *Daily Telegraph* in the UK had presented a promotion of their website at an advertising conference in Dublin in 1995 in Jurys Hotel, Ballsbridge. This became known as 'the event in the tent' among the attendees of advertising and media personnel; despite a howling wind outside and the rattling of the tent, the display was impressive, even awe inspiring.

Managing director Kieran Walsh was then encouraged by the IDA and *The Irish Times* to visit a newspaper exhibition in America. The potential of the internet was revealed with speakers from the UK *Guardian* and *The Chicago Tribune*. Many technical specialists from Microsoft and Netscape were there.

Through a family connection, Kieran stayed a week in the United States, visiting internet designers, who recommended books on html plus design graphics and people to talk to. *The Irish Times* also helped with contacts.

The website was launched n 1996, and soon the *Munster Express* was getting congratulatory e-mails from as far away as Australia, New Zealand, the USA and UK, where the web was adopted earlier than in Ireland.

Susan Doxey and Catherine Costello were involved in the website from early on, with Paul Wright of Waterford, formerly of Ireland on Line, assisting; eventually, with some help from the telecommunications and software group TSSG in Waterford Institute of Technology, the website expanded.

Mediaforce in Dublin are handling digital national advertising for *Munster Express* as well as national display advertising including Heineken, Murphys Stout, Hibernian Aviva, Aer Arann and Telecom companies. They have proved very successful over the past decade. But as with similar newspaper sites across the world, a successful business model is still being sought.

US ambassador Jean Kennedy Smith visited Wateford several times during her term of office. During her 1993 visit she spent time in the Munster Express *office watching the paper being laid out.*

Hospital in the news in the 1990s

Major construction work on the Waterford Regional Hospital in Ardkeen, to replace the old Ardkeen Hospital, began in 1987.

The Ardkeen Hospital originally opened in 1952 as a 240-bed chest hospital specialising in TB. The hospital was built on the site of Ardkeen House which was one of the series of extravagant houses built in the 1860s by the Malcolmson family.

With the support of the then Minister for Health, the late Dr Noel Browne, who was born in Waterford, the capital cost for the hospital had been obtained largely from the Irish Hospital Sweepstake fund. The original hospital, known as the Chest Hospital Wing of Sub-Regional Sanatorium at Ardkeen, comprised six separate units where a total staff complement of 130 cared for 240 patients.

Construction of the new hospital began in 1987 and continued on a unit by unit basis until the mid-1990s. As the decade began, the hospital was full due to a national flu epidemic. Expansion in January 1990 allowed new patients to be transferred from the old hospital in the grounds into the new building. This was followed by moving paediatric patients in 1991.

Overspending problems hit progress in the hospital in 1991. Controversially, admissions had to be curtailed. An industrial dispute erupted, with workers complaining about the reduction in beds and the fact that patients were often being asked to carry out chores. During the dispute the four major hospitals in the county, including Waterford Regional Hospital, were subject to picketing. ATGWU district officer Walter Cullen called for all 36 medical and psychiatric facilities in the county to be picketed, while Seán Kelly, the union president, intensified

The old Infirmary building vandalised

pressure on the health board by criticising the government body for not engaging in direct sit-down talks with the union on the issue.

Industrial action was to return sporadically throughout the first half of the 1990s. At this time, the hospital began to concentrate on providing a top-class surgical service—£30,000 was raised for new surgical equipment through voluntary efforts. The next industrial problem was a work to rule sanctioned by the Irish Nurses Organisation (INO), which sought to limit the extra duties not included in their work contract that nurses were being asked to carry out.

The dire need for reduction of waiting list times for vital surgery was highlighted during the middle of the decade. Thanks to much lobbying, a host of developments were announced, including the hiring of six new consultant surgeons (and a training school with a high calibre junior staff). These improvements only arrived after a heated political battle. With the hospital bolstered with these staff;the centre became the premier orthopaedic facility in the country.

Albert Reynolds opening the new Port of Waterford in 1993

A dredger in the port

A £2.3m investment in the construction of an acute psychiatric unit added to the Waterford Regional Hospital's prestige. Around the same time, the paediatric ward received praise for its efficiency.

Minister of State at the Department of Health Brian O'Shea announced a £1.5m injection to improve obstetrics facilities and a new epidural service for mothers, and other improvements, including new beds for the regional ENT service, were ushered in.

The middle years of the 1990s saw more industrial action, with the cleaners and dental workers initiating sit-downs and picketing.

As the decade progressed, hospital activity increased by 6 per cent each year for a three-year period without equivalent increases in funding. The hospital was forced to cut costs and pursue efficiencies. As a result of this programme, Waterford Regional Hospital moved into the 2000s as one of the premier hospitals in the country.

The former Celtworld building later became a nightclub called South and later a shopping arcade.

The offices of the Munster Express *mourning the death of longtime Editor J. J. Walsh*

End of an era

Newspaper veteran J. J. Walsh (born 21 December 1905) was still working part time up to the year 1990, after over 60 years in the business. With him now were various family members, including his son, future Editor Kieran Walsh. The newspaper was still highly rated, though the challenge of local radio was on the horizon. These were changing times for the media but also for J. J. Walsh whose period at the helm was coming to an end.

In 1991, failing health began to affect him and his pace of life slowed down for the first time. He was now 85 and was still playing golf and writing editorials. As his wife used to say to the family, he intended to die in harness. But time was against him and he eventually died of melanoma, a cancer that is hard to escape when you get to that age. That summer he missed his first Olympics since the War. His

J. J. with golfer Severiano Ballesteros

J. J. Walsh on the Great Wall of China

daughter Priscilla flew the family flag there in Barcelona and later became a director of the company.

He was to die the week the Kilkenny hurling team won the All Ireland. He passed away in Dublin on 10 September 1992 having been discharged from St Vincent's Hospital to a nursing home.

The next edition of the *Munster Express* carried the story of 'HUGE FUNERAL FOR ESTEEMED EDITOR' on the front page, with a picture of staff members escorting the coffin past the offices where he had worked for so many years. Inside the paper, five full pages surrounded by a black border described his long and active life, and his intensive involvement in the sporting, historical and charitable aspects of Waterford life.

In an obituary, news editor John O'Connor vividly evoked the sometimes stormy management style of J. J. Walsh and carefully demolished two inventive Waterford legends: firstly that J. J. always carried a small salt cellar to sprinkle on his shoulders in an attempt to fool people that his quite obvious wig was genuine; and second that there was a 'black list' of names that he would not allow to appear in the paper.

On other pages were pictures of J. J. with various international sports characters, with politicians such as Conrad Adenauer of Germany and Charles Haughey, with the Irish Olympic team in San Francisco and on the Great Wall of China. Tributes from President Mary Robinson and Taoiseach Albert Reynolds headed an impressive list of local bodies expressing their sorrow at his passing.

Two years later, journalist Michael Bance wrote a colourful biography of 'Smokey Joe' Walsh, in which he attempted to justify his view that Walsh was 'one of the most outrageous characters in the world of Irish provincial journalism'. The book was not reviewed in the *Munster Express*.

Mrs and Mr Stephen O'Flaherty, Volkswagen franchisee, former British Prime Minister Ted Heath and J. J.

Award for Myriam Walsh

All five of J. J.'s children worked in the *Munster Express* at one time or another. Myriam worked as a travel writer and Dublin correspondent in the 1990s. In 1993 she was presented with the Spring Award of the CCE (Conseillers du Commerce Exterieur) medal for journalists by the sponsors Servier(Ireland) Industries, at their company premises in Arklow, Co. Wicklow.

The medal is awarded as part of a new Award Scheme for journalists writing articles about France. The scheme is organised by Les Conseillers du Commerce Exterieur de la France, a group of nine French businessmen managing French companies based in Ireland. Members of the CCE are appointed by the French government and each bi-monthly medal is sponsored by an Irish-based company.

The medal is awarded to encourage newspaper articles about France. It was devised in recognition of the strong economic and commercial links between France and Ireland and the interest shown by Irish journalists in various aspects of France. Myriam's winning article, on Normandy, was entitled 'Normandie, la crème de la France'.

The article went forward to the finals together with the five other bi-monthly writers competing for the award of best article of the year. Kate Holmquist, feature writer with *The Irish Times,* was the eventual winner of the trophy. The *Munster Express* was in good company!

'Spraoí, a Gaelic word meaning 'celebrate' or 'party'

Not only did the meaning of the word Spraoí perfectly describe the very essence of what Spraoí was to become, but it also rhymed perfectly with the first festival in 1993! Decision made! Print the poster!

The idea back in 1993 was simply to have some fun and perhaps a little madness on a summer Sunday. This initial idea materialized as a one-day event, held on the streets of Waterford city. It was so successful that the idea grew; perhaps it could become an annual summer festival in Waterford? Thus began it all.

And what has since developed is one of Ireland leading arts companies, Spraoí. Now, with over sixteen years work in the area of spectacle, outdoor theatre, event management and festival production, Spraoí has amassed a vast wealth of specialist skills and experience. In 2002 the company embarked on an ambitious project—to construct its own studios, the first purpose built building in Ireland dedicated solely to the development of street art. With the support and assistance of the Arts Council of Ireland, Waterford City Council, other grants and public

donations, Spraoí achieved this dream, and moved into its new and permanent home at Carrickpherish, Waterford, in January 2003.

Spraoí is perhaps best known for the annual Spraoí Festival which takes over the city centre of Waterford for the entire August Bank Holiday weekend, and which now attracts audiences in excess of 80,000 people to the city.

Spraoí concentrates on showcasing top quality national and international street art and world music. Spraoí's own production, The Spraoí Parade, is now a major highlight of the annual festival, involving approximately 300 participants, with large scale floats, costumes, props, lighting and special effects.

The annual Spraoí festival in full swing

The Fleadh Mór *by Michael Dower*

Waterford man Vince Power came home for a visit in July 1993 and brought with him over sixty top Irish and international music acts for the Fleadh Mór on Tramore Racecourse. The two-day event showcased the talents of an extraordinary range of performers from Ray Charles, Joan Baez and Bob Dylan to more contemporary groups.

The Saturday gig featured Soul Reazon, Energy Orchard, Runrig, Maria McKee, The Pogues, and the legendary Jimmy Cliff, who brought Jamaican reggae to Tramore in brilliant sunshine.

Van Morrison was his usual arrogant and brilliant self. Christy Moore and Ray Charles closed the show with a natural backdrop of a full moon reflected in the calm bay with thousands of sunburned bodies swaying to the rhythm.

In the Mean Fiddler tent on the Saturday were Tasmanian Dust Devils, Draoícht, Speranzo, Andy White, Vinny Kilduff, Lindisfarne, A Woman's Heart, John Prine and Moving Hearts.

A view of the crowds at the Fleadh Mór

On the NME stage were Puppy Love, Bomb, The Kevins, The Flaps, The Shanks, The Tulips, Grin, Rare, Lir, Emperors of Ice Cream, The Power of Dreams, Simon Carmody's the Golden Horde.

On Sunday the Mean Fiddler stage kicked off with Miss Brown To You, Katel Keining, Sold at Louis, Hank Wangford, Bhundo Boys, The Funkin Barstewards, Mary Coughlan, Luka Bloom, The Chieftains.

The NME stage held the Color Party, Ringer, the Mary Janes, the Grasshoppers, Sack, LMNO Pelican, Tony St James, Bird, Big Geraniums, the Pale.

On Sunday the main stage opened with the Glam Tarts, Cry Before Dawn, The Frames, Shane McGowan and The Pogues, Sharon Shannon, all time rock and folk great, Joan Baez, the Hothouse Flowers, and Van Morrison, who broke into giggles during 'Brown Eyed Girl'. Van was followed by a great show from Bob Dylan, known for his hit and miss performances over the years—this was one of his hits. The main stage closed on Sunday with Jerry Lee Lewis.

This two day event wasn't the success everybody had hoped for financially but musically was a 'winner all right'.

The Forum

The Forum, Waterford, originally opened as the Regal Cinema in 1937 and operated as a 1,500-seater cinema up to the 1970s, after which Bingo became its main activity. Extensively refurbished during the 1980s, it was transformed into a 1,200 seater modern concert hall, which opened as the Forum in April 1990.

The following decade it played host to top touring acts including Johnny Cash, The Corrs, David Gray, Van Morrison, Christy Moore, Billy Connolly, and many more. During the millennium year major renovations again took place to create a multi-purpose venue with four separate spaces with capacity ranging from 100 to 1000.

Catering to both young and old, the Forum, Waterford, offers diverse entertainment weekly and since reopening, in October 2000, has been host to the very best of Irish and international musicians, DJs, comedians and theatrical productions as well as running bingo sessions.

Joan Baez

The 2000s

Waterford Crystal

In its edition of 4 April 1947 the *Munster Express* announced a momentous event for the city. A new glass factory was opened.

The original Glass House was founded in 1783 by George and William Penrose. Though it quickly became famous for the clarity and precision of virtuoso craftsman- ship in the faceted cutting of lead crystal, it folded in 1851 as a result of competition from England.

The continuing fame of the name attracted a courageous post-Second World War revival. This revival yielded stunning benefits for the city and country for fifty years, and another stunning and deeply unhappy experience when bankruptcy overtook the enterprise in January, 2009.

The revival in 1947 is credited to Charles Bacik, a Czech whose glass factory fell victim to the war in Europe.

Aerial view of modern Waterford

(above) Lismore Suite (below) a craftsman blowing Waterford Crystal

Encouraged by a former customer, Bernard Fitzpatrick, a Dublin jeweller, he sought refuge in Ireland. The factory started off by importing low quality soda glass from Belgium and making simple engravings on them. The elaborate glass factory producing high quality engraved heavy crystal glass, using craftsmen blowers and working on molten glass in furnaces, was some way off.

The following decades marked important phases in the story. The 1950s saw the back-breaking work of revival, recruiting staff, melting crystal to standard, developing a cogent product range, finding markets and finance.

The latter came from the Irish Glass Bottle Company (IGB) and two dynamic executives, Noel Griffin and Hans Winkelmann, in 1950. They became joint managing directors, one an accountant, the other with technical expertise. IGB was run by members of the McGrath, Duggan and Freeman families who had made their money in the Sweep.

Spectacular achievements were realised in the 1960s, not least the blending of experienced Continental glass workers imbued with a disciplined work ethic and a growing cohort of young, willing and talented local workers. The integration worked well and the new enthusiasm fired people like Miroslav Havel, design, and Con Dooley, sales, to deliver consummate success in their fields. Waterford, the people and place, had powered upwards to re-engage with the legendary brand name.

After a marathon US marketing trip, Con Dooley reported huge demand: 'It's no longer a sales problem, it's a production problem.' The answer was more expansion at the Johnstown factory, and later the development of the colossal Kilbarry complex whose scale belied an intimate concept of hand-craft.

The 1960s were tinged with sadness with the untimely death in 1965 of Dr Winkelmann in a sailing tragedy.

Growth was immense to the point where an American business expert opined in 1972 that, should this growth rate continue, the 'Waterford' business would be bigger than the United States by 2000!

The company, now public, became the darling of the stock market, every shot a goal. Surplus funds were tempted into acquisitions such as retail stores, motor distribution, postcard production, and in quick time the company had become a conglomerate.

Another bad blow was the death in a drowning accident off Dunmore East of the dynamic managing director Noel Griffin in 1981. This traumatic event led to management by a group of four, Paddy and Seamus McGrath, Owen Kealy and Colm O'Connell. Within a few years, the McGrath family relinquished control to London-based Globe Investments who engaged Paddy Hayes of the Ford Motor Company, as chairman and group chief executive.

Three major developments ensued to deal with a number of competitive issues undermining crystal. There was the acquisition of Wedgwood, efforts to lessen dependence on the US market and divestment of non core businesses.

The first significant redundancy programme was introduced following which Globe's interest declined, leading eventually to control by the Tony O'Reilly/Goulandris party. Dr Paddy Galvin of Guinness was brought in to run the Waterford manufacturing company and introduce further down-sizing moves which resulted in a 14-week strike in 1990.

When that retrenching phase ended, Redmond O'Donoughue took over, followed by John Foley—marketeers had succeeded engineers in running the crystal operation. The millennium provided a welcome boom but underlying problems remained, compounded by changing tastes in the marketplace and competition from cheaper imitation product. The introduction of new

Pleasure cruiser off Waterford

designs, continuing outsourcing of product, combined with redundancy programmes and significant cash injections from Tony O'Reilly and Peter Goulandris did not prevent decline, despite the fame of the brand, rivalling, some said, world class quality marques such as Rolls Royce and Harley Davidson. In 2005, the Dungarvan factory was closed with the loss of 500 jobs. Nonetheless, the receivership announced in January 2009 was unexpected.

Snowcream—the end of an era?
by JOE FALVEY

In July 2008 the 50-year-old Snowcream milk plant in Glenville closed its production. It had been a key player in the local agri-food business and provided significant employment on and off site. At the close there were 50 employees. In former times, the company employed as many as 120, not counting independent agents known in the trade as 'doorstep agents' who distributed up to one-third of production.

The late 1940s and early 1950s were bleak times here in Ireland yet it was during these years that two of Waterford's best known companies were established, Waterford Glass and Snowcream. Two different traditions of skill and processes and indeed, background, one resonant of the urban industrial, the other of rural pastures, yet both sought to enhance different natural products.

The Snowcream story began back in 1952 with the first depot and offices at Thomas Hill, in the heart of Waterford city. It really had its genesis some while before that when the late Johnny Aylward met Kurt Kraus, then a refugee from war-torn Europe. Kurt, who for many years has resided at Newtown, was a qualified refrigeration engineer, a rare skill in Ireland of that time. This chance encounter in the People's Park led to the establishment of Southern Refrigeration and Icecream Co.

Hitherto, milk distribution had not been rationalised in any way and followed simple age-old patterns of direct selling by the farmers to shops, hotels, hospitals, even directly to houses. Snowcream was founded to deal with local dairy farmers and to distribute milk in an organised and systematic fashion. Against the background of the scourge of TB the old unhygienic practices could not be

allowed to survive. Pasteurisation became essential, which meant that there was a rationale for a middle man between the farmer and the customer.

With Johnny Aylward and Kurt Kraus on that first pioneering board were fellow directors the late Don Sheedy, Billy Kervick, Dick Tilson (finance officer) and law adviser Dr R. Counahan. Parts of Dublin were the first to be provided with pasteurised milk, but Waterford was next with pasteurised milk from Snowcream. This was long before it was compulsory to supply pasteurised milk. Snowcream, indeed, pioneered other good practices long before they were the norm in their industry.

Johnny Aylward was a remarkably astute businessman, tough when necessary but always a gentleman and straight in his dealings and a considerate employer. The farmers formed an association of Waterford and district producers

The old Waterford Paper Mills, Granagh, plant, now used as industrial units. Nearby is Dawn Meats, another strong local business.

Clover Meats closed on the early 1980s leaving hundreds out of work. The factory was later bought by Larry Goodman's Anglo Irish Meat Co.

to deal collectively with the company, to negotiate prices, supply contracts and ensure quality. A minute book of 1956 reveals regular business meetings of the Snowcream board with such farmers as J. O'Neill, R. Walsh , Sean O'Donovan (Kilcohan), David Veale (Dunhill) and Michael Hayes (Orchardstown).

Initially, customers were suspicious of pasteurised bottled milk, fearing that the natural product had been interfered with. The company had to convince doubters of the benefits of pasteurisation and the dangers of untreated milk. In time, Snowcream got the message through and their market grew.

During the 1950s business grew to such an extent that a bigger depot and processing plant became essential. By 1961, the company had completed their move to the present site at Glenville. The 10-acre site there had been acquired from Sir Ernest Goff for £3,000, Around this time the Wexford Creamery became part of the company and later in the 1960s, so did Snowcream Midlands at Moate

Flahavan's oat mill in Kilmacthomas, Co. Waterford

(the latter became detached at a later date). In 1973 the Waterford Co-op was founded, and Snowcream became a part. In 1988 that enterprise became a PLC and in 1997 merged with Avonmore. A new corporate image and branding came with the name 'Glanbia' in 1999.

Production grew by 50 per cent at Glenville over fifteen years to 2000 with approximately 9m gallons being collected, processed and distributed throughout the entire South-East annually. However, by the time Avonmore and Waterford Foods merged in the late 2000s, it was becoming clear that Snowcream was too small to compete in an era of multi-nationals and giant plants.

Hurling success in the last decade
by DERMOT KEYES

There may have been no All-Ireland senior hurling titles claimed by the men of Waterford since the county's re-emergence as a serious contender in 1998, but these past dozen years have been golden. Kilkenny, Cork and the re-emerging Tipperary may have monopolised the roll of honour since 1999, but no county has outstripped the Déise in terms of drama, emotion and entertainment in this still young century.

Five trophies have been lifted by Waterford captains in the past nine eventful seasons. Until 2002, Waterford had featured in only five Munster deciders between 1966 and 1998. For a young generation of Waterford supporters, the bad old days of the 1970s and 1980s are as alien as having no more than two TV channels to choose from and a tape deck on your sound system.

The new optimism has clearly impacted on the fortunes of De La Salle, Coláistí na nDéise and Blackwater College in colleges' hurling in recent seasons. Even in Tramore, hardly a traditional hurling scene, provincial honours have been gained at schools' level—perhaps the greatest legacy the Flynns, McGraths and Shanahans of this era will ultimately reflect upon.

The current All-Ireland under-14 champions wear white and blue and defeated Kilkenny to claim the Tony Forristal title at Walsh Park in the summer of 2010. That may not have been a win which earned too many national headlines, but defeating a team in black and amber for a hurling trophy could prove priceless within a short number of years.

Under Gerald McCarthy, structured training and the experience of a five-time All Ireland winner on the sideline made a team with many stylish players, but a lack of cohesion, into a solid, reputable unit. Under Justin McCarthy, the skills engendered by Gerald were translated into three Munster Championships, a National League title, which featured a series of magical battles against Cork.

Of those, the 2004 Munster final ranks as arguably the greatest provincial decider of them all. Ken McGrath's majestic leap and fetch above the redeployed Diarmuid O'Sullivan was the towering moment of a magical 70 minutes.

That the stirring 2004 and 2007 Munster finals weren't matched by Liam MacCarthy Cup success was crushing. Then, of course, there was the player heave against Justin McCarthy in 2008. So exit Justin, enter Davy Fitzgerald, a younger man, equally driven but with a differing ethic on how the game should be played.

It is to the Sixmilebridgeman's credit that he has built a Munster title-winning team out of the ashes of the team slaughtered by Kilkenny in 2008 . And he'll get another crack at the big one come the 2011 Championship—we'll all be watching.

Up the Déise.

The new Rice Bridge under construction as steam rises over Cherry's Brewery, Mary Stree

The Sport of Kings

by DONAL BARRY

The annual August Race Meeting at Tramore is the highlight of the racing calendar in the Waterford and general south-east area. It has provided many happy memories for racegoers and those who built their annual summer family holidays around the race festival. It has been an important event for the local tourist industry and in particular for hoteliers and bed and breakfast owners in Tramore.

Racing in Tramore can be traced back to racing on the beach in 1785. It became so popular with the locals that a six-day meeting was held there in 1807 in mid-August, a tradition that continues to this day. In 1888 a race committee under Martin J. Murphy renovated the facilities and revived the racing. However, the course and facilities were in constant danger from stormy seas, and in 1911 the course was so badly breached that time had to be called on the event. Undeterred, the racecourse company established a new course at Graun Hill on the outskirts of Tramore, where the present course is situated.

The 1983 English Derby runner-up Carlingford Castle was galloped the 'wrong way round' at Tramore before-hand in preparation for the big race. The reason his trainer Liam Browne did this is because going left-handed at Tramore closely resembles (on a smaller scale) the unique gradients of Epsom Racecourse. The horse nearly brought off a famous Irish win but Teenoso and a certain Lester Piggott were just too good. A total of €5m was spent on a complete refurbishment of the racecourse under the new ownership of local racing enthusiasts.

Since then the venue has gone from strength to strength with much emphasis placed on providing entertainment for racegoers after the meeting. Another piece of history was made on 1 January 2000 when the first race meeting of the new millennium in Europe was held in Tramore attracting a record crowd of 11,000. This race, The Mean Fiddler Handicap Steeplechase, was won by No Problem, trained in Cork by Gerard Cully, owned by Tommy Cronin and ridden by Waterford jockey Shay Barry. On 1 January 2002 Tramore was the first racecourse in Europe to use the euro currency and the Wilf Dooley Handicap Steeplechase was the first listed race at the track.

In December 2006, Waterford County Council granted permission for a multi-million euro racecourse on a 183-acre green site at nearby Lisselan. The 1 mile, 4 furlong 80 metre wide, left-handed track, will accommodate chase, national hunt and flat racing. A two-storey 30 metre glass-fronted stand to accommodate 10,000 people will be constructed. Within the grandstand complex, there will be a multi-purpose hospitality area, seating 300, with panoramic views of the entire racecourse and the parade ring. The racecourse development at the new location is currently on hold but track has already been laid.

Dunbrody Abbey, quays, Waterford

The Munster Express office seen through the rigging of a tall ship

Martin Cullen

One of Waterford's most successful modern politicians, Martin Cullen, was forced by illness to resign in March 2010.

Originally elected to the Dáil as a PD in 1987, he became Mayor of Waterford, as his father and grandfather had been, in 1993–4. He later joined Fianna Fáil and became Minister for State in the 1997 coalition.

After the Government's re-election in 2002, Cullen joined the Cabinet as Minister for the Environment, Heritage and Local Government. This was good news for Waterford, since a local TD had not been in the Cabinet since Austin Deasy in the 1980s. The new minister faced tough decisions and emotional issues. Zealously pursuing opportunities for Waterford, Cullen managed to ensure many vital improvements to environmental problems and infrastructural projects in the city during his tenure. During this time, the minister oversaw and opened expansive £18m government buildings at the Glen in Waterford, in addition to lobbying for the North Quays project.

Cullen received much local recognition for his efforts on behalf of the city, notably winning the newly created

Dockside scene, with artwork by Gottfried Helnwick on the Odlum flour mills building

been troubling him for months. On 21 January 2010, he published his speech to the Forum on Defamation Law, in which he spoke of his experiences of false allegations of adultery in the press. Cullen described how he had been pursued by the media, with reporters harassing him, photographers following him. On one occasion a photograph of him, the Taoiseach and his secretary, and a third man at a state function, was altered to make it appear he was dining alone with the woman. He recounted how his sons suffered bullying at school defending his honour.

Although his departure left the local Fianna Fáil party with a problem in defending its second seat in the constituency, the general verdict was that Martin Cullen had been good for Waterford. As *Munster Express* political commentator Dermot Keyes put it: 'His eight years as minister have been credited with shoe-horning up to €2b for the south-east; even his political foes will acknowledge that he never stopped beating the drum for Waterford within Government.'

Tower Hotel excellence award for his extensive efforts in lobbying for the EU environment ministers to hold meetings in Waterford during Ireland's EU presidency in 2005, as well as the Tall Ships race, also held in 2005.

In 2004 Martin Cullen became Minister for Transport, hugely raising Waterford's profile. During his time as minister, from 2004 to 2008, he played a key role in a number of major road projects, including a new bridge and bypass in Waterford city, an extension of the ring road and the Waterford to Dublin motorway. On a national level he oversaw improvements in Iarnrod Éireann services, the privatisation of Aer Lingus and a huge extension of the motorway system in Ireland.

In 2008 he became Minister for Arts, Sports and Tourism and continued in this position until March 2010 when he resigned both his ministerial appointment and his seat in the Dáil, citing a back problem that had

Mayor Martin Cullen with Spraoí drummer

Night of nostalgia at the Theatre Royal *by* KIERAN FOLEY

The history of the *Munster Express* was fondly recalled by all those who took to the stage at the Theatre Royal on Thursday 7 October 2010 to celebrate the legacy of the paper. Marking the momentous 150th year milestone, much reminiscing took place at the special gala evening, and the esteem with which the paper continues to be held was very much evident to all.

Managing Director and Editor Kieran Walsh spoke with Waterford broadcasting legend Eddie Wymberry about the history of the paper, and its significance in the lives of all its readers. Kieran Walsh, third generation of the Walsh owners, spoke of the impressive circulation area which the paper had built up, incorporating south Kilkenny, south Tipperary, south-west Wexford as well as Waterford city and county. He described the proud bipartisan stance which his father ensured was evident in the newspaper. 'The paper always gave a level playing field to all parties,' he said.

Asked by Eddie Wymberry how his father would feel about the current political and economic turmoil Ireland finds itself in, Mr Walsh said the late J. J. Walsh would be angry and would feel that politicians had lost control. He affectionately recalled his own introduction to the *Munster*

Munster Express staff and some retirees in party mood after the 150th show in the Theatre Royal

Express, remembering the hard work which he saw his father carry out, often working throughout Christmas. Kieran Walsh said he was always fascinated by the history of the *Munster Express* building on Hanover Street, especially the bullet holes in the old newsroom, caused by shots fired from Mount Misery during the Civil War, which can still be seen today. The sporting loves of J. J. Walsh were recalled, including his love for boxing. He was also an avid fan of the Olympic Games, and his involvement with the 1956 Melbourne Olympics was especially recalled, as he was one of the first to report on Ronnie Delaney's historic win. 'He was a man that always followed the flag,' said son Kieran. 'He believed sport was the way countries should compete, not war,' he added.

Eddie Wymberry spoke of his own friendship with J. J. Walsh. He mentioned the former editor's sense of humour,

the natural ease with which he could speak in public without a script, and the tremendous profile he had among newspaper people. Mr Wymberry noted that the *Munster Express* always seemed to 'mop up' the advertising market. When asked how the paper managed to attract so much advertising, Kieran Walsh said the paper provided readers with what they wanted, in turn attracting loyal advertisers. 'We serve them, they serve us,' he said. Saying that the *Munster Express* always strived to raise issues and highlight injustices, Mr Walsh stated: 'We champion the area.'

MC Nichola Beresford, who spoke of the importance of the *Munster Express* as 'a social document,' introduced another *Munster Express* legend, 'a name synonymous with the paper', News Editor John O'Connor. Mr O'Connor spoke of the difficulties which newspapers, including the *Munster Express*, now face, but added that he believed

Munster Express *MD Kieran Walsh with Mr & Mrs Pat Robinson. Pat is a descendant of the Fisher family, founders and original owners of the* Munster Express. *On Pat's left is Roswith Walsh, Director of the* Munster Express *and Myriam Walsh.*

there would always be a place for newspapers. 'There will always be a place for fair and accurate reporting' he said, highlighting the trust with which people view the *Munster Express*.

Mr O'Connor paid tribute to staff, both past and present, especially those who had adapted from the methods of typesetting used in the 1960s, to the advanced computer software now in use. 'The last fifty years saw momentous change,' he said. He likened the pace of change to 'learning to ride a bicycle, then a fast car, then a spaceship.' He added that it was 'a great credit to the staff that we got through. There were times when we were perilously close to losing editions, but we didn't,' he said. Saying the paper was fortunate to have the staff it does, he congratulated all who had served on the *Munster Express* ship down through the years, and wished Bon Voyage to those who would do so in the future.

The Mayor of Waterford Councillor Mary Roche said she appreciated the contribution the newspaper has made, and continues to make, to Waterford. She said she first became aware of the significance of the *Munster Express*, when working with Red Kettle, realising the important role it played. 'Whether it's the front page, obituaries, or looking for a new job, the *Munster Express* plays a central role,' she said. 'The *Munster Express* has always helped with campaigns in Waterford, such as the fight for university status,' she added.

Munster Express reporter Dermot Keyes interviewed Waterford senior hurling legend Ken McGrath on stage. The sporting star confirmed the important role the paper plays. 'All the lads look forward to opening the *Munster* every week,' he said.

In summation, Kieran Walsh thanked his family, readers, advertisers and staff, for their continued support.

One hundred and fifty years of technology at the *Munster Express*

- 1860 *Munster Express* founded, to cater for farmers and country people. Several newspapers were published in Waterford at the time. The paper is set cold by hand from cases and printed on a Columbia. This technology (though in iron) would have been recognisable to Gutenberg and Caxton.
- 1882 Death of Joseph Fisher, the first proprietor. His sons take over. Twenty years later they sell out to Edward Walsh, a local businessman.
- 1898 First purpose-built newspaper office on the Quay.
- 1907 Walsh combines all his newspapers in face of the threat from William Martin Murphy's *Irish Independent*.
- 1912 First Linotype hot metal typesetter installed.
- 1920 Printing now done on a Wharfedale flatbed; the typical run, 5,000 copies.
- 1930s News stories begin to appear on the front page.
- 1930s Gaelic font installed in Linotype.
- 1938 J. J. Walsh, the editor/proprietor, takes Seán Lemass' warnings of wartime shortages seriously and invests heavily in newsprint which enables him to last out 'The Emergency' and even make paper available to other publishers.
- 1950 The Cossar, a reel-fed flatbed machine installed.
- 1957 Electronic engraving is introduced.
- 1965 Six linotypes now employed, also TTS line printer setters.
- 1975 Photon Photocomposition installed.
- 1976 Web offset Linotype Pacer installed; paper printed part letterpress and web offset for one year.
- 1977 Single colour Solna press bought from Sweden.
- 1989 Colour satellite bought from Linotype.

- 1993 News pictures in colour on front page for the first time.
- 1994 Direct input agreement with unions. Photon phased out and laser setting introduced.
- 1995 Proprietary electronic make-up programme. ISDN installed.
- 1996 International presence: website established and e-mail connection initiated with stringers.
- 1996 New press bought from the Isle of Wight adds to colour capacity.

- 2004 Page make-up shifted to InDesign.
- 2002 Press bought from *Leinster Leader* capable of 6 pages of colour per 16 page section.
- 2005 Single vb/wcol print eliminated.
- 2005 Web quad colour system from the US installed.
- 2005 Manual computer to plate system installed.
- 2007 Web leader quad bought from Scotland, capable of perfecting 16 pp colour in one pass; the old press sold to Malaysia.
- 2007 New automatic computer to plate system.

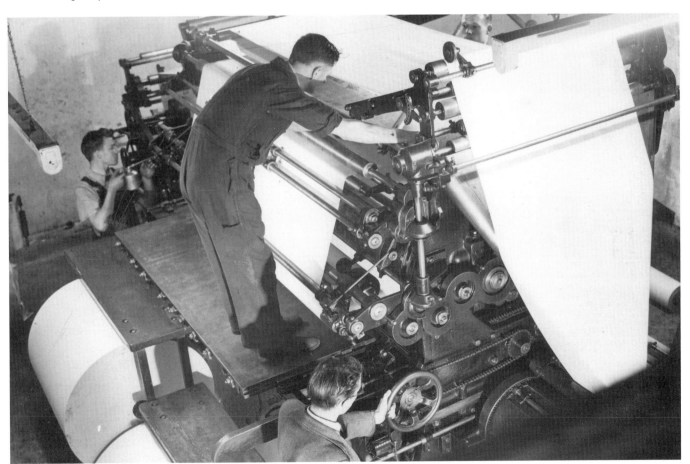

Jack Kennedy, machine minder, feeds the Cossar Press with a reel of newsprint

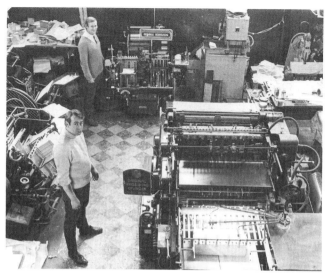

Michael Jinks Walsh and Frank Jacques in the machine room

In the press-room: in the foreground is Mick Flannery an All-Ireland hurling winner in 1959. Behind him is Jack Kennedy and to his left Nicholas Walsh.

Making up the paper in the composing room: Butch Power, Tony Rogers, Harry Condon, Des Hodge, Paddy Gallagher, Michael Dower and Michael Comerford